The Present Personal

The Present Personal

PHILOSOPHY

AND THE

HIDDEN

FACE OF

LANGUAGE

HAGI KENAAN

COLUMBIA UNIVERSITY PRESS
NEW YORK

COLUMBIA UNIVERSITY PRESS
Publishers Since 1893
New York Chichester, West Sussex
Copyright © 2005 Columbia University Press
All rights reserved

Library of Congress Cataloging-in-Publication Data

Kenaan, Hagi.
The present personal : philosophy and the hidden
face of language / Hagi Kenaan.
p. cm.
Includes bibliographical references and index.
ISBN 0–231–13350–2 (alk. paper)
1. Language and languages—Philosophy. I. Title

P107.K46   2004
302.2'24'01—dc22   2004056036

Columbia University Press books are printed
on permanent and durable
acid-free paper.
Printed in the United States of America

c 10 9 8 7 6 5 4 3 2 1

To Vered Lev
the secret of a rose's heart
my love and admiration

Contents

Preface ix

Introduction: Philosophy and the Personal 1

CHAPTER 1
Language and the Bell Jar 19
   1. A Picture Held Us Captive 20
   2. Language's Frame 25
   3. The Fact of the Propositional 28
   4. "This Is How Things Are" 33
   5. The Bell Jar 37

CHAPTER 2
The Limits of Language and the Dream of Transcendence 41
   1. Philosophy and Disappointment 41
   2. Language: The Map 44
   3. Language and Silence: The Example of Abraham 50
   4. The Limits of Language and the Question of Freedom 53
   5. Before the Law of Language 58
   6. From Disappointment to Philosophy 60

CHAPTER 3
Austin's Fireworks 65
1. Austin's Fireworks: The Promise of the Pragmatic Turn 66
2. How to Do Things with Austin 69
3. The Act of Speech 72
4. The Pragmatic and the Personal 79
5. The Mirror at Hand: Afterthoughts 84

CHAPTER 4
Personal Objects 87
1. Heidegger (Before) and (After) Austin 87
2. Heidegger's Pragmatic Interpretation of the Ordinary 90
3. The Prison of the Ordinary 95
4. The Aesthetic Elision of the Personal 97
5. Van Gogh's Shoes 102
6. Sabina's Hat 111

CHAPTER 5
Language Unframed: Beauty as Model 125
1. It's Funny 127
2. Aesthetic Judgment 135
3. The Language of Taste 138
4. The Phenomenality of Your Words 140

CHAPTER 6
Personal Time 149
1. The Time Is Past 150
2. Time and the Language of Possibility 153
3. Time Prefaced 159
4. Perhaps Present 168
5. In My End Is My Beginning 174

Epilogue 177

Notes 183
Index 193

Preface

The Present Personal was written in Tel Aviv between 2001 and 2003. These opening years of the twenty-first century failed to fulfill any of the hopes raised by the advent of a new millennium. Living in Tel Aviv, in Israel, it has been impossible to alleviate or even pretend to alleviate the darkness of this period, one during which violence, hatred, intense human suffering together with the growing indifference toward the suffering of others have become the form of daily life.

This period has not been a very conducive one for the writing of a philosophy book. Indeed, *The Present Personal* was composed in— and despite—an atmosphere that ultimately renders any form of reflection not specifically connected to the political context irrelevant, a situation in which the need for radical and even subversive action on the part of individuals is so pressing that it threatens to leave the engagement with humanistic work bereft of any genuine value.

The Present Personal is a philosophical attempt to think the depth of the possibility of listening to the other person. This ethical possibility belongs to the heart of our human interaction, and yet it typically remains so inconspicuous and undemanding that philosophy can ignore it altogether, as if it did not exist. This possibility is referred to in this volume as the *personal* although other terms—such as the *singular* or the *idiosyncratic*—are also useful. In writing this book I have been motivated by the belief that by listening to the personal we could make our world a better place to live in.

I shall remember the writing of this book as an essentially solitary experience. This is probably not news. At the same time, I was also most fortunate to enjoy the constant support and help of friends, family, teachers, colleagues, and students.

Karsten Harries, who was my adviser at Yale ten years ago, has encouraged me ever since to carry on the difficult search for a style of thinking that I could call my own. Since generosity comes so naturally to Harries, I'm not sure he knows just how important this encouragement has been for me over the years. Ran Sigad was my most influential teacher during my undergraduate studies at Tel-Aviv University. In addition to his lasting friendship, I wish to thank him for his careful reading of this manuscript and for the way in which, sensing that I needed to let go of it, he decided very much against himself to spare me the pointed edge of his criticism.

My mother, Nurith Kenaan-Kedar, her husband Benjamin Z. Kedar, and my brother Jonathan Canaan have always been close, constant, and loving companions. My father, Gabriel Canaan, did not live to read this manuscript. I wonder if it would have appealed to him. I am not sure. However, before his death, before the book was underway, I did have a chance to read to him a few pages that now appear in chapter 6. In recalling his response, I greatly miss him.

I am delighted to thank my ten-year-old daughter, Ilil, who is every bit as special as her name and definitely the most marvelous girl I know.

The support of my friends was invaluable to the writing of this book. It was so invaluable, in fact, that I can only hope I am more successful in expressing my gratitude to them in private. Nevertheless, I wish to acknowledge several significant discussions that were formative to my work. These include a long conversation with Ariel Meirav while wandering the city during the course of an afternoon that turned into evening, a late-night conversation with Yaron Senderowicz at a bar, a conversation with Eli Friedlander alongside a pond, another conversation sparked by Leora Bilsky saying "I only now realize that this life is mine," a talk with Wayne Froman at a Chagall exhibition, and a conversation with Vered Lev Kenaan while sitting, next to each other, on a plane—clouds around us. To her I dedicate this book.

There were other conversations that were significant at various stages and junctions in the writing of this book: dialogues with my friends Gabriela Basterra, Simon Critchley, Hanoch Dagan, Dan Daor, Ilit Ferber, Ron Katwan, Lior Levi, Noa Naaman-Zauderer, Joel Pearl, and Eli Stern. These friends read sections of, and sometimes all of, my manuscript while being themselves intensely engaged in projects of their own. I am grateful to them for their illuminating and helpful responses.

The philosophy department at Tel-Aviv University has provided me much more than just colleagial support. I would especially like to thank Shlomo Biderman and Zvi Tauber. I deeply thank Yehonatan Maor, Jessica Moss, Emily Wittman, and Michael Zakim, for their engaged and insightful suggestions for improving the manuscript. It is to Emily Wittman's imagination, in particular, that I owe the title of this book, *The Present Personal*. Special thanks are due to Wendy Lochner of Columbia University Press, whose enthusiastic response to and warm welcome of the book meant a lot to me. I also thank Susan Pensak for her sensitive editing of the final manuscript.

The Present Personal

Introduction:
Philosophy and the Personal

1.

In making a beginning, this book needs to overcome a certain difficulty. Unlike many philosophical books that have the privilege of simply plunging into a given question or of naturally making a move on a map they take for granted, this study belongs to a family of philosophical texts whose subject matter is not yet charted by philosophical discourse and whose central questions need time in order to resonate as questions at all. *The Present Personal: Philosophy and the Hidden Face of Language* is concerned with a dimension of the experience of language that, for different reasons, cannot call attention to itself within the horizons of the investigation of language carried out by either Anglo-American or Continental philosophy. Somewhere in between Anglo-American and Continental perspectives on language, there is a hidden lacuna—a blind spot that marks our inability to recognize the depth of the connection between our experience of language and our experience of persons.

How is the speaking individual present in language? How do you inhabit your language, or, in what way is it *you* who inhabits the language that you speak to me? In what sense are you there "in" the words you utter? What is the relation between your singularity as an individual and the general and public structure of the language you use?

The relationship between everyday language and the speaking subject is articulated in fundamentally different ways by Anglo-American philosophy of language and Continental thought. Yet, despite these differences, in both traditions the understanding of this relationship typically takes the form of a general presupposition all too readily taken for granted that, as such, levels the depth of the above questions and ultimately severs the crucial tie between our relation to language and our relation to others. Consequently, philosophy today is indifferent to the question of listening. Philosophy seems unable to illuminate for us the possibility, the event, the situation, of listening to the speech of the other person. And it cannot help us in the search for genuine forms of listening to each other. But is this something philosophy should be able to do?

2.

What do I listen to when I listen to you? I listen to you.
What do I hear when I listen to you? I hear you.

These postulations can be understood either in a trivial or a nontrivial way. When you speak I can listen to what is being said by you. At the same time, I can also listen to you saying the things you are saying. I can listen to and hear what *you* say. The possibility is there for me to hear *you*. To put this in another way, when we speak I can avoid listening to you. But even if I do listen to the things you say, to the words and the sentences that you utter, even if I understand the contents of what you are saying, I may still not be listening to your speech, to what you are saying. The possibility is there for me to listen to what you are saying without actually listening to *you*. When philosophy thinks of language, this difference between "what you say" and its apparent double, "what *you* say," typically goes unnoticed or else is dismissed as insignificant. This is at least partly the case because the individual's presence in language seems to mean nothing more than the obvious fact that when speech occurs there must necessarily be someone who functions as a speaker—you, in this case. However, the obvious fact that speech involves a speaker hides a more evasive kind of presence that is not merely factual: how is a speaker present in speech? What concerns us, in other words, is a dimension of language that eludes us precisely because it cannot be articulated as a fact. This might help us to understand why this focal point of speech typically remains so inconspicuous and so undemanding of philosophy that philosophical considerations of language can ignore it altogether, as if it did not exist. Indeed, when you speak nothing forces us to hear or become attentive to your presence in the things you say. Nothing appears to change significantly if we remain indifferent or deaf to the manner in which the "you who speaks to me" inhabits what he or she says. We may remain just as deaf as John Marcher, in Henry James's *Beast in the Jungle,* who lives his life without ever hearing the love expressed through the words of Mary Bartram. John Marcher continually fails to hear that her language speaks love to him. He is unable, or perhaps unwilling, to listen to the manner in which Mary's love reverberates again and again in the things she says. This deafness lasts a whole lifetime, or at least until it is too late.

The presence of the singular individual in what he or she is saying is indeed elusive. Yet this elusiveness is particularly symptomatic of the kind of philosophical reflection that addresses language without ever developing an ear for it. Language must be listened to, but when thinking philosophically about language we so often misplace our capacity to listen. On the whole, it would not be wrong to say that philosophical queries about language are not distinguished by a musical ear. Philosophy is experienced at admiring and resenting language, in celebrating, renouncing, and even manipulating it, but it has rarely succeeded in simply being intimate with language. This intimacy is, in my view, a necessary condition—or, in Heideggerian terms, a necessary mood, albeit a mood that Heidegger has not appreciated—for encountering the speaking of language.

Hence the central aim of *The Present Personal* is to show how language can be listened to in a manner that allows the singular presence of the speaking individual to become part of our daily life with language. The book seeks to recover the philosophical possibility of listening to language as the embodiment of a speaker's idiosyncratic, unique presence. It explores this possibility by identifying and articulating an existential focal point at the very heart of ordinary meaning. I term this focal point *the personal*. At first sight, the personal might not be easy to recognize, but once recognized it will necessarily change our perception of language much in the same way that a face appears in a completely new light when we reveal pain or sadness in a smile or the way a painting can unexpectedly take on a new form once we discover in it the presence of a hidden anamorphic image. When we uncover the personal, it becomes clear that we can no longer sustain the common oppositions between the commonality and singularity of meaning, between structure and freedom in language, and between the epistemic (or semantic) core and the aesthetic effects of the spoken.

Even more important, by developing a philosophical ear for the manner in which the spoken embodies the idiosyncratic presence of the speaking individual, we will take a necessary step in attuning ourselves to both the ordinary and the metaphysical source of language's meaningfulness. Our path will lead us closer to a fundamental dimension of meaning that brings language to life and marks it with what Wittgenstein calls a "physiognomy." Responding to the physiognomy of language, we can take a cue from Levinas and think of the appearance of the personal in the light of the appearance of meaning in a human face. The experience of the personal in language is similar to the kind of looking that allows us not only to see "that you are happy" or "that you are crying" but also "to see you happy," "to see you crying."

This analogy with the human face suggests that the question of meaning is anchored in the nature of the encounter between you and I and cannot be understood independently of it. It suggests that the appearance of the meaningful is not rooted in the representability of the factual order but in our being, in the ways in which we exist for one another. At the same time, however, we need to be careful when we compare language with the human face. Unlike a human face, language is not the kind of entity that calls us to relate to it through its singularity. In fact, the very possibility of a meaningful language seems to depend on our ability to forget the singularity of the linguistic event and to embrace it as a token of an abstract form of meaning. The meaningfulness of everyday language ultimately appears independent of both the singularity of the actual reverberation of one's words and of one's singular existence in language. In other words, language seems essentially indifferent to the singularity of its speakers. And it is with this seeming indifference that the analogy to Levinas's human face ends. Language, unlike Levinas's human face, has no inherent resistance to reification. On the contrary, it appears to demand that philosophy objectify its workings. Yet, when we treat language in this way, when we construe our philosophical engagement with language solely on the basis of its objective appearance, we are mistaken. Indeed, we could even say that we are committing an error. If this formulation invokes certain ethical connotations, this is because I do indeed consider the present investigation to be ethical at heart. The uncovering of the personal will show how the ethical is inherent in the appearance of meaning and how the question of the unfolding of meaning in language is ultimately integral to the question of the good life.

The personal grows between us. But the fact that it resides there between us does not mean that the personal in itself assumes the form of a fact. On the contrary, the personal dimension of language disappears when it is handled as a fact. In the tenderness and fragility of its form, the personal resembles a flower much more than it resembles an objective fact; the personal appears and blossoms, but it also closes up and withers. And again, like a flower, the personal is also easily destroyed when not properly attended to. This vulnerability is one of the major difficulties we face in the attempt to take hold of the personal. This, however, is where philosophy so often stumbles when it thinks about language. There is something in the structure of the philosophical encounter with language that suppresses the personal. But why does this occur? Why does philosophical reflection on language elide the presence of the personal? In what sense can thinking be said to conceal that which it reflects upon? And how does a reflection ultimately occlude that which it reflects on?

3.

In the initial stages of my work I had assumed that this problem was confined to the philosophy of language in the Anglo-American tradition. As a student of the philosophy of language, I always sensed that there is something crucially important that never gets addressed, that gets systematically repressed by the intelligent, sophisticated, and often witty philosophical language game to which I tried to adapt myself. But for many years I was unable to understand the source of my dissatisfaction or comprehend why that philosophical framework deserves to be called a prejudice that needs to be called into question in the first place. In other words, I was unable, within the parameters of the philosophy of language, to envision the possibility of an "outside," of an alternative that would justify my discontent and guide or support a possible departure. This is, of course, a very frustrating situation. You feel imprisoned and yet you see no walls around you. Is this the kind of captivity Wittgenstein has in mind when he speaks of showing the "fly the way out of the fly-bottle"? I can think here, for example, of a child who grows up in what seems to be the perfect home, a home in which everything is nice and pleasant, where discussions are unprejudiced and open, where everything is clear and conspicuous; there are no secrets or forbidden topics and, nothing—absolutely nothing—is excluded from what may be said. Nevertheless, the child finds himself feeling deeply constrained and suffocated by something he cannot name. How can he—and from a different perspective—how dare he be so miserable in such a perfect setting?

Today I understand that my inability to see what the philosophy of language systematically effaces was more than my own shortcoming. It results as well from a kind of double censorship which the philosophy of language exercises as it sets the stage for thinking about language: Anglo-American philosophy of language not only censors the personal, it also obliterates all signs of this censorship. In Anglo-American philosophy of language as well as its extension in the philosophy of mind, the question of the tension between the singularity of a speaker and his or her language is never foregrounded. In fact, there is no way to even raise this question, because the public structure of language is posited as the ultimate (the given, the desired, the necessary and the only conceivable) condition of the individual. For the philosophy of language, being an individual self is equivalent to having the form of an intelligible self. Moreover, since the being and the intelligibility of the individual completely coincide, the singularity of the individual is made ineluctably dependent on the public form of the intelligible. In other words, the individuality of a speaking subject can only announce itself in the form of a fact that belongs to a global factual order: the order of the intelligible, the order of the "we." Robert Brandom, for example, posits the task of "telling who or what we are" as an essential move in setting the field for the "investigation of the nature of language." His influential *Making It Explicit* thus begins by unquestioningly embracing the "we" as the prior grounds for thinking (or, we might say, not thinking at all) about the individual's place in language. For Brandom, the singular existence of a speaking self can ultimately mean no more than the fact that that self belongs to the "one great community" of the "we," that it can "be correctly counted among us." That is, for Brandom, "taking or treating someone as one of us may be called recognizing that individual."[1]

The internalization of a universal "we" as the ultimate horizon for our understanding of the singularity of the speaking individual typically goes hand in hand with a cognitive appropriation of the essence of our being in language. According to Brandom,

> We are distinguished by capacities that are broadly cognitive. Our transaction with other things and with each other mean something to us in a special and characteristic sense: they have a conceptual content for us, we understand them in one way rather than another.[2]

For Brandom, the essential form of meaning in language is the form of conceptual, or propositional, content, and consequently he identifies the key to human involvement in language as the very capacities that enable an abstract "language practitioner" to participate in the "social practices that distinguish us as rational, indeed logical concept-mongering creatures—knowers and agents."[3]

The cognitive framing of the question of meaning is not, however, a philosophically innocuous move. It is a consequential move that preemptively qualifies and ultimately distorts the character of the field of speech by determining one, and only one, definite standard for language's meaningfulness. In the philosophy of language, the form of propositions has established itself as the fundamental form of the intelligible and functions as the ultimate standard of our attachment to language. Regulated by the ideal structure of cognitive judgment or, alternatively, the structure of information, the hegemony of the propositional is already operative at the preliminary stage in which philosophy structures its discussion of the phenomenon. Hence, in commonly thematizing language as—to use McDowell's words—the "sharing of knowledge" or the "instilling of information,"[4] the philosophy of language inevitably forces the phenomenon of meaning into a factual structure. In this view not only is the inner form of language's meaningfulness taken to be the depiction of facts but the actual appearance of meaning is also, in itself, understood as a kind of fact whose proper expression is, in turn, the form of a proposition. However, by systematically giving priority to the propositional, the event of meaning is unavoidably reconstructed as essentially independent of the horizons of the relationship between you and me. Insofar as it is constituted as a uniform and self-sufficient object, propositional content is necessarily indifferent to the claims of an individual's existence. It is a self-identical form of meaning that is neither temporal nor perspectival and completely foreign to both the character of the contingent and the possibility of transcendence. In other words, content is a form of meaning that is, in principle, unaffected by the tongue, breath, voice, body and idiosyncratic being of the individual who speaks. It is divorced from our particularity and has no connection to the manner in which you, being who you are, inhabit your speech. In the philosophy of language, speech is impartial and unerringly the same for whoever uses it (governed perhaps by the same laws that regulate the circulation of currency). Indeed, language is perceived to be always available for anyone's use. Nevertheless, it remains completely external to the particularity or peculiarity of our intrinsic attachment to our words.

In the philosophy of language, language bears no mark of the fact that, when you speak, it is you and not just anyone in your position who is its singular speaker.

But, what would it mean for us to recognize and respond to the affect of individuality in language? Can the individual be brought back to language in a genuine way?

4.

The task of uncovering the personal is an endeavor that must necessarily develop hand in hand with an understanding of the philosophical tendency to elide it. This book's primary diagnosis articulates this structural deafness in terms of a predominant philosophical tendency to embrace the structure of (propositional) content as an ultimate model for the unfolding of meaning. The internalization of the form of propositions as the standard of the intelligible leaves the personal understated. It would not be wrong to say that the personal is the *under*stated. The personal is what hides (itself) when language states (itself). The personal is covered up by the linguistic structure of stating, by the manner in which assertive, fact-depicting language posits itself at the heart of meaningfulness.

The philosophical elision of the personal is a symptom of the hegemony of propositional form in philosophy's encounter with language. However, in exploring the close relationship between the elision of the personal and the hegemony of the propositional, *The Present Personal* reveals it to be symptomatic of not only the Anglo-American philosophy of language but, more surprisingly, of Continental approaches to language (from Kierkegaard to Heidegger to Derrida), whose opposition against the hegemony of the propositional results, as I argue, in alternatives that actually recreate philosophy's indifference to the personal. Whereas Anglo-American philosophy of language is indeed a philosophy of content par excellence, it is interesting to see that this tendency to conceptualize speech as the transmission of semantically structured content between agents is not specific to the philosophy of language. And that the narrow and instrumental telos of this standard philosophical setting, together with the essential externality of the relationship between a language user and her language, is characteristic also of Continental discourse. In other words, although the leveling of the experience of individuality is clearly manifested in central trends in Anglo-American philosophy of language, it is also characteristic of Continental perspectives on language (from existentialism to poststructuralism), albeit for completely different reasons, which this book will explore. In schematic fashion it would thus not be wrong to say that, despite fundamental differences between the Anglo-American and the Continental approaches to language, neither tradition makes room for the presence of the individual, qua individual, in the language he or she speaks. In both traditions the singularity of the speaker is ultimately irrelevant to what language conveys. And, language, in turn, is understood in a manner that ultimately leaves no trace of the individual's singularity.

To be more specific, we may point here to a peculiar kind of mirroring at work in the relation between Anglo-American and Continental perspectives of language. One way to describe this mirroring is to say that, while Anglo-American philosophy erases all traces of the tension between being an individual and being a speaker of a language, Continental philosophy—beginning with its existential currents—accentuates this tension in a manner that leads to what Blanchot paradigmatically calls the "antagonism between language and the singular."[5] While Anglo-American philosophy completely sublimates the individuality of the so-called language user, Continental philosophy construes the possibility of genuine individuality in direct opposition to language. This opposition can be found, in different ways, in both existential critiques of language and in poststructuralist critiques of subjectivity, both in the existentialist's attempt to "rescue" the individual subject from the averageness of linguistic meaning and, on the other hand, in the postmodern attempt to release the construction of meaning from the constitutive authority (e.g, intention, desire) of an individual subject.[6]

Another way to put this is to say that while the Anglo-American and Continental traditions both adopt Hegel as the father of their reflection on language, they respond very differently to this Hegelian heritage, one tradition remaining obedient while the other rebels. More specifically, although both traditions internalize the Hegelian understanding of language as a manifestation of the conceptual, universal, public (and simultaneously all encompassing) structure of the intelligible, they part radically when it comes to interpreting the significance of this structure of intelligibility.

Hence, if we look back, for example, at how Kierkegaard grapples with the totalizing effect of the Hegelian system, we see that, in calling upon us to resist the domination of the universal, Kierkegaard's basic understanding of language remains confined to the parameters of the Hegelian notions of *Geist* and *Sittlichkeit*. Kierkegaard shares the very assumption that he finds so problematic, and it is precisely because he accepts Hegel's public and general vision of language that the problem of the individual becomes so acute for him. In other words, what gives rise to Kierkegaard's preoccupation with the problem of realizing individual existence, and what ultimately makes this authentic possibility a paradox, is his recognition that the intelligibility of human experience necessarily grows from a shared social matrix of meaning and that language (the most explicit manifestation of that matrix) is constitutive of who we are as individuals. For Kierkegaard, individuality is a project that must be undertaken in spite of language.

As we consider the trajectory leading from Kierkegaard (and Nietzsche) through Heidegger to the French existentialists, we see that the core of this picture of language basically remains intact. For Heidegger, everyday language is one of the clearest manifestations of Dasein's absorption in the public averageness of the "they." In *Being and Time*, the Publicness of *das Man* "proximally controls every way in which the world and Dasein get interpreted," and under this control in which "everything ... gets passed off as something familiar and accessible to everyone"[7] any possibility of a genuine relation of the self to its own being is leveled. Individual existence has no place in the public realm of intelligibility. Furthermore, what complicates the possibility of freedom or the individuation of the self is that the "they" is not something imposed on Dasein from the outside. The "they" does not dominate the self as an external force. Rather, it "belongs to Dasein's positive constitution." The "they," in other words, is not only what separates the self from the possibility of authenticity, it is also what constitutes the possibility of selfhood in the first place. "The Self of everyday Dasein is the they-self."[8] And in this context the language of everyday Dasein, the language that allows the meaningfulness of Dasein's world to open up, is the average language of the "they." It is a medium or a condition of intelligibility without which, analogously, there is no selfhood. Yet, at the same time, it is a condition in which the authentic self is systematically effaced. For Heidegger, therefore, the possibility of authenticity is necessarily dependent on a particular modification of our common, linguistically structured forms of meaningfulness. But because the kind of intelligibility prescribed by the "they" is not so much an option for Dasein as much as it is the basis for the meaningfulness of content as such, authenticity cannot in itself be discovered in any new, or alternative, domain of meaning or in any other kind of language or conceptual scheme for that matter. Whatever kind it is and whatever form it may adopt, content is always a product of the "they" according to Heidegger. Hence, since the very structure of content necessarily excludes the singular presence of the individual from language, the search for authenticity must therefore imply a turn of the self to the place of no content.

Thus, while Anglo-American philosophy of language is the ultimate paradigm of a content philosophy, or a philosophy of content, Heidegger's philosophy—and perhaps Continental philosophy more generally from Nietzsche to Freud to Derrida—may be understood as a thought against content, a philosophy of discontent. At the same time, however, it is crucial to observe here that these diametrically opposed perspectives nevertheless both internalize the very structure of content as basis for reflection on language. And thus, although the hegemony of the propositional in twentieth-century philosophy is most clearly apparent in Anglo-American philosophy of language, it is often just as dominant in Continental approaches to language. And again, this is because the opposition against this hegemony not only tends to internalize it as its starting point but also often results in alternatives by which the propositional continues to reign through its negative reproductions: much like a photograph and its negative image.

Hence, taking a slightly different example, we may notice that when Marcuse criticizes in *One-Dimensional Man* the philosophy of language of his day, he is not suggesting that this philosophy is unfaithful to the phenomenon of ordinary language but completely accepts the accuracy of the picture described by Anglo-American philosophy. According to him, this philosophy, "in its exactness and clarity . . . is probably unsurpassable—it is correct."[9] And yet this philosophy must be criticized because of the manner in which it reproduces the "the prevailing universe of discourse and behaviour."[10] That is, for Marcuse, the problem with the philosophy of language lies in the manner in which it internalizes the prevailing logic of domination. The philosophy of language is, according to him, the kind of discourse that not only conceals its own ideological character but also systematically delegitimizes the possibility of the Negative and therewith the source for an alternative logic of protest.

The point that interests us, however, is that despite his criticism against the philosophical absorption in ordinary language, Marcuse shares with the philosophy of language an understanding of the essence of ordinary speech. And thus, although he rightly criticizes the kind of "positive thinking" that is "pressed into the straightjacket of common usage,"[11] the starting point for his critique evolves from a particular vision of that "language of John Doe and Richard Roe . . . the language which the man on the street actually speaks," which is, in itself, not different from the manner in which it is depicted by the philosophy he criticizes.

Echoing Heidegger, Marcuse's critical relation to the language of the everyday exemplifies how Continental philosophy is often too quick to accept the dullness and averageness of the ordinary as the basis for its reflection on language. Marcuse calls upon us to transcend the "language of John Doe and Richard Roe." But should we, in the first place, allow the anonymous "language user" or the "language practitioner" to become the model for our daily life with language? Should we really understand ordinary language as the "language which the man on the street actually speaks"? Who is this anonymous "man on the street"? Doesn't he or she have a name of his or her own? Doesn't he or she carry that name (just as they are tied to the word *I*) in a manner that is not all anonymous, but, rather, personal?

5.

The search for the personal is a search for a possibility that lies at the heart of our experience of language. This is the possibility of an encounter that occurs within the very texture of language: an encounter with the singularity of a *you* who speaks to me. With this end in mind, the book's starting point cannot be located within the horizons set by the philosophy of language, but necessitates an opening of language in a manner no longer dominated by what Marcuse understands as positive thinking. Language cannot be understood exclusively in terms of its facticity, because the facts of language not only teach us who we are but also conceal from us what we can be. Ordinary language is never only what it is. It is always also indicative of what it leaves outside and what it refuses, for a variety of reasons, to articulate for us. Our point of departure in *The Present Personal* is this very recognition that the sphere of everyday language is our home, but also the condition and place of our captivity.

Unlike Anglo-American philosophy, the Continental tradition acknowledges the limits and limitations of the intelligible with a distinctive ambivalence that gives rise to a range of different response patterns. The Continental tradition contests the structural limits of language in a variety of ways, through gestures of transcendence, protest, subversion, and irony—from silence to paradox to poetry (and then back again to forms of silence, etc). However, despite their ostensible differences, these forms of response share a crucial assumption that what can be expressed and heard in ordinary language is necessarily bound by language's structural limitations. That is, language's structural limitations are taken to impose an impassable boundary upon us, a horizon beyond which the silent reverberation of singularity will never find expression.

Sartre, for example, sees language, by definition, as a sphere in which "subjectivity experiences itself as an object for the Other,"[12] a sphere that cannot provide authentic communication. Blanchot, on the other hand, embraces the poetic as a means to encounter the uniquely subjective, precisely because he agrees that men ordinarily communicate "through what they have in common, and consequently through what is exterior to themselves." For Blanchot, "if it is true that men communicate only insofar as they communicate what is absolutely unique to them, it is laughter, tears, the sexual act, rather than the workings of language, that would offer them the means to unite with each other in an authentic communication."[13] Yet Blanchot also sees the possibility of retrieving what everyday language takes away from us through the transgression of the ordinary. For Blanchot, the poetic is the attempt to "withdraw from language the properties that give it a linguistic meaning, that cause it to seem language by its assertion of universality and intelligibility." Or, in the words of Valéry, whom Blanchot follows, "poetry is the attempt . . . to restore by means of articulate language those things or that thing that tend obscurely to express cries, tears, caresses, kisses, sighs."[14]

In spite of a certain reluctance to use the word *authentic* here, it would nevertheless be right to say that "authentic communication" is the central issue of this book. However, unlike Blanchot or for that matter Heidegger, the move I wish to make will not take us away from everyday language, nor will it imply a transcendence of the horizons of content. Instead, I wish to come closer to the richness, complexity, and depth—should we use the word *mystery?*—of the ordinary. In contradistinction to the prototypical understanding of everyday intelligibility as a necessary form of captivity, this study searches for singularity and freedom in the heart of the everyday, arguing that the limits of ordinary content provide the necessary condition of freedom and singularity. Hence, as we search for the personal, it is not enough for us to identify the delimiting effect of language's propositional structure. We must also free ourselves from the temptation to totalize the effect of language's limits and thereby turn our critique of these limits into yet another and perhaps more dire form of captivity. The idea that the structure of everydayness is a form of captivity is often more captivating than the average forms of everydayness themselves. The ordinary is not our prison. We become the prisoners of the ordinary only once we internalize the opposition between our freedom and certain dominant structures of the everyday. Although the structure of language can indeed be said to bar us from the personal, we must also remember that language is the very place where the personal shows itself. Language is the form that conceals the personal, but it is also through language that the personal resonates.

6.

The book's search for the personal moves through three stages. It begins with an examination of existentialism's discontent with the propositional structure of language, continues with the implications arising from the overthrow of language's propositional form, and, last, arrives at my own solution to uncovering the personal. Hence, I open with Kierkegaard's existential critique of language, which makes it clear why the propositional structure of language does not allow the spoken to reflect the singularity of the self. And yet, as I show, this existential protest against language's effacement of the individual too easily evolves into a new form of conceptual captivity, one that internalizes the limits of language as a given necessity. The self is left facing the apparently immutable structure of language, and all it can do, as Wittgenstein puts it, is "run up against the limits of language." In our search for the personal, such a position is not an option.

The second part of the investigation examines the twentieth-century reaction against the propositional, focusing on two outstanding attempts to subvert the hegemony of content: the pragmatic turn of J. L. Austin and the poetic path of Heidegger. Once again, however, these two radical conceptions of language ultimately offer a negative lesson. In spite of their nonpropositional vision of language, the trajectories they open for philosophy remain removed from and external to that ordinary reverberation of language within which the personal speaks. This is because the personal lives in the heart of our human attachment to content and cannot be encountered if we understand content only as a limiting factor. Content not only determines the conditions of our captivity in language, but, as suggested, also provides a home for us.

Guided by Kant's *Critique of Judgment* and by phenomenology, the book's third part addresses the very experience of listening to the personal. The personal lives in the tension that exists between a person's language and her individuality, a tension that escapes any external understanding of the relation between language and the individual, the public and the singular. The personal is the pulse of the intimate attachment by which the individual and language are related, a pulse that cannot be measured but can be heard. As, for example, when you use a word that you cannot bear or when you say "Mom" or "Dad" and they are no longer there. The personal is the umbilical chord that nurtures our being-in language: it is a living tissue that sustains a position for us in the public sphere of language, but it is also that by which, as individuals, we remain riveted to our words in a contingently singular manner. The personal is like an old scar that, for the external viewer, is no more than a fact among facts, yet one that, in the hands of the old maid Euryclea, pulsates as the very root of recognition: isn't this you, Odysseus? The personal is the hidden face of language.

CHAPTER 1
Language and the Bell Jar

The personal tends to hide itself from philosophy's reflective gaze. It resists the collecting movement—for Heidegger the original sense of logos—that enables thinking to take in the world as thinkable. In remembering how Heraclitus speaks of nature, we may even want to say that the personal likes to hide (itself). However, this is only partially true. The other side of the story is that philosophy makes it difficult for the personal to show itself: it hears the intelligibility of everyday language in a way that stifles its resonance. This is not the result of an occasional deafness as much as it is a symptom of a structural condition—a form of entrapment—characteristic of how theoretical thinking situates itself in relation to language. There is something in the structure of our encounter with language that hinders us from encountering the personal, that suppresses the personal, and that leaves it understated. What is the structure of the relationship between philosophy and language that keeps the personal from being heard? What is the structure of a reflection that does not allow its source to appear? In what sense can thinking be said to conceal what it reflects upon? Indeed, how can a reflection hide what it reflects? And, more generally, what exactly would it mean to understand philosophy's thinking about language as a form of entrapment?

1. A Picture Held Us Captive

Let us begin thinking about these questions with the help of an important section in Wittgenstein's *Investigations*. In *Philosophical Investigations* §115, Wittgenstein writes as follows,

> A picture held us captive. And we could not get outside it, for it lay in our language and language seemed to repeat it to us inexorably.[1]

Wittgenstein speaks of "us" as being held captive. The context of this captivity is not self-explanatory. But since this passage is found at the heart of several sections in the *Investigations* that address the character—the tasks, limits, and illusions—of philosophy, we may assume that the "us," or the "we," to which Wittgenstein refers is the us engaged in philosophy. Instead of opening up the world to us, our philosophical reflection—unexpectedly?—places us in captivity.

By thinking philosophically we are held captive. This may seem to be an oxymoron and, in fact, the captivity that concerns Wittgenstein constitutes an interesting inversion of the prototypical philosophical structure of captivity that we know so well from Plato's allegory of the cave. In contrast to the captivity of the Platonic prisoners, one resting on their immersion in (a narrow domain of) immediacy, the problem for Wittgenstein lies in the way we are immersed—the way we position ourselves—in reflection. For Wittgenstein, it is the philosophical, or the reflective, condition—or, at least, its dominant version—that bars us from freedom.

The possibility of emancipation for the prisoners in Plato's cave has a different trajectory than the one concerning Wittgenstein. Yet, at the same time, we may also note that Wittgenstein's concern is not completely absent in Plato. In particular, it finds an echo in the second part of the cave allegory, with the philosopher's, the ex-prisoner's, return to the cave. That is, in the end the question for both philosophers is how to return. For Wittgenstein, this question is made particularly relevant in the face of a condition of (entrenched) reflexivity that prevents us from encountering our freedom, that does not allow the meaningfulness of things ever to become an expression of our freedom.

According to Wittgenstein, what specifically administers our philosophical captivity is a picture, a picture that governs the shape and horizons of our thinking. Given the context of Wittgenstein's concerns, we may say that he is taking issue here with a picture of language: a picture of language whose presence in language ultimately bars reflection from opening up to language. The term *picture* is not coincidental here. As in the case of Plato's allegory, the captivity of which Wittgenstein speaks is not a result of false beliefs but of an attachment to an image. What holds us captive is something that shows itself. However, in using the term *picture* instead, for instance, of such terms as *conception, thesis,* or *theoretical model,* Wittgenstein indicates that the kind of trap that concerns him cannot be understood in strictly cognitive terms. Our entrapment is not a form of conceptual confusion (as, for example, in Ryle's "category mistake"). Unlike clear assertorial cognitive positions, the meaningfulness of pictures is typically manifested in a nonthematic fashion. And unlike the ostensible neutrality informing the intelligibility of theoretical statements (i.e., we can understand the meaning of a statement, or entertain a thought in the Fregean sense, independently of our position in regard to it), the meaning of pictures is never free of an affective dimension. Another way to put this is to say that when a picture captivates us it does so by dominating our imagination rather than our intellect—and this also explains why, in the *Investigations,* Wittgenstein's primary confrontation is with a "picture of the essence of human language" belonging to a childhood memory rather than any well defined philosophical position.[2]

The picture constrains us. "We could not get outside it." But do we at all know what and where the picture's outside is and what it would mean to get there? Does the term *outside* have any meaning for the prisoners in Plato's cave? I think that what makes the picture so captivating is that it does not call attention to itself in the form of a picture. The picture does not appear to us as a distinct framed object. It is never simply there in front of us, and so cannot become our *vor*stellung. We are unable to see the picture as a picture. Instead, the picture holds us "in," supplying the topography as well as the horizons of the confines within which we find ourselves, the confines by which our seeing becomes possible in the first place. That is to say, we are not only held captive by a picture we cannot see, but our inability to see and represent the picture—our inability to establish a distance necessary for recognizing the picture as a picture—is precisely what holds us captive. In other words, appearing to have no boundary or definite limit, the picture regulates our captivity by concealing the possibility of an outside. The picture—like the shadows on the cave's wall—can hold us captive precisely because we do not (and do not know how to) experience it as a limit or a limitation.

The picture is the form of our attachment to what we can see. This means, however, that its captivating effect is twofold. The picture not only hides from us the very fact that it is bounded, but it does so through a particular manner of giving itself to our gaze. The picture can hide its limits (its form of depiction) because our gaze is fixated on its contents. To be more specific, philosophy is held captive by a picture whose form of depiction of everyday language conceals its own evolution from everyday language. Turning to everyday language as an object of reflection (as the content of picture), philosophy tends to suppress the manner in which everyday language grounds its reflective turn. Philosophy internalizes a picture that forces it to turn its gaze away from the roots it originally had in everydayness. This is a picture in which everyday language can only appear in the form of a fully constituted object, one that bears no trace, no memory, of its own passage into reflection.

The picture, in other words, does not provide an incorrect depiction of language, but rather a partial depiction that hides its partiality. Wittgenstein tells us that the picture "lay in our language." Indeed, it can be found in our daily routines with language. It is imprinted in our handling of ordinary language, in much the same way that, speaking our "mother tongue," we literally make a place for the speech of our mother. It can be "read" from the phenomenon but—just like the musical score that lies in our singing—it cannot begin to do justice to it. The picture cannot contain the complex heterogeneity and richness of the life of our language, of our life with language, but, at the same time, it tends, nevertheless, to dominate our perception of language. According to Wittgenstein, the picture perpetuates itself through language. Language is said "to repeat it to us inexorably." This repetition—which is both the regulating mechanism and the symptom of our captivity—is structurally not very different from its psychoanalytic counterpart in which a repetitive fixation issues from our inability to integrate the meaningfulness of an event or an image into experience. What holds us captive is a picture for which we have failed (for we do not know how) to find a proper place in the space of reflection. This picture continually reasserts itself because we cannot see it as a picture as long as the language of reflection takes its rapport with everyday language for granted.

In other words, language becomes the source of our self-perpetuating captivity because of the way we use it in reflecting on language. That is, we use language in positing language as a philosophical subject matter, but we do so while turning our back on our ordinary, prethematic attachment to language. Our reflection on language—the language of our reflection on language—typically effaces its own roots. And as it loses touch with the roots from which it grew, language can return to meet itself only in a very narrow form. For when reflection forgets the home it originally had in language, it returns to language as a stranger. And, when it returns to the home of language as an outsider, it can only see what outsiders see (when facing a home): a picture. Moreover, since this picture forces itself upon reflection in that no trace is to be found of its outside, it no longer appears as a picture at all but as the thing—language—in itself.

When reflection forgets its home in everyday language, it looks at language as a person who examines (the features of) his face in the mirror without accepting the face he sees as his own, and, furthermore, without embracing what he sees as a uniquely human face. This kind of reflection may be exact and perceptive. But, as Sartre and before him Nabokov show so well (in their unloving first-person descriptions of the face), the correctness and precision of reflection are, in themselves, insufficient for responding to that which makes the human face different from an inert expansion of flesh.

Hence, the picture typically takes hold of us as we approach the point from which we hope to see things as they are. A temptation awaits us at the entrance to reflection, the temptation to see the mirror image of things instead of the things themselves. Indeed, we may say that the picture, of which Wittgenstein speaks, is the mirror image of language. (Why are we so attracted to mirrors? Is it because mirrors allow us to focus on ourselves, while forgetting that we are ourselves?) To put this differently, we may say that captivity in the hands of a picture is typically a symptom of a philosophy that takes its own beginning for granted. It is a symptom of a form of thinking that depends on ready-made answers to the question of how to begin, or how to encounter the presence of language, or, again, how to return to the ordinary.

In putting things in this way, we are in a position to see that Wittgenstein's passive construction of the "us" held in captivity may also be somewhat misleading. According to Wittgenstein, "a picture held us captive." But can we understand this captivity as a condition that is merely forced upon us by reflective language? Does this captivity simply happen to us because of the nature of language and reflection? And, consequently, should we follow Wittgenstein in understanding the way out of captivity as "a battle against the bewitchment of our intelligence by means of language"?[3] The notion of "bewitchment," just like the passive formulation of our role in captivity, may too easily allow us to forget that language is not an independently given condition that happens to affect us. Wittgenstein's image of captivity may seem to suggest that our entrapment in language can be understood independently of the ways we treat our language. But this is misleading: we are never uninvolved bystanders in relation to our language. Emancipation cannot be achieved through "a battle against" the influence of language, because we are always implicated to begin with. We are active participants in the administration of our captivity. Our complicity is there for all to hear: we are the masters of the language that holds us captive.

The implications of this complicated structure of captivity and emancipation will be elaborated only in the following chapter. At this point, however, we still need to explain further how a philosophical picture of language can conceal our language from us. More specifically, what exactly is in the form of our reflection that bars us from responding to the actual unfolding of everyday language?

2. The Frame of Language

Again, Wittgenstein is helpful here. In *Investigations* §114, in the section that immediately precedes the image of the captivating picture, Wittgenstein critically responds to a statement he himself had put forward in the *Tractatus*. He writes:

> (*Tractatus Logico-Philosophicus*, 4.5): "The general form of propositions is: This is how things are."—That is the kind of proposition that one repeats to oneself countless times. One thinks that one is tracing the outline of the thing's nature over and over again, and one is merely tracing round the frame through which we look at it.[4]

This passage shares with §115 its basic imagery. While in §115 we are held captive by a "picture," in §114 our attachment to "the frame through which we look" prevents us from engaging the nature of things. Furthermore, in both passages captivity finds expression in the form of "repetition." While in §115 "language seemed to repeat [the captivating picture] to us inexorably," in §114 it is a certain kind of general proposition that "one repeats to oneself countless times."

What makes §114 specifically relevant to our discussion is that it underscores the connection between our captivation in language and the rule of propositions in our thinking about language. Wittgenstein articulates the problem of philosophy's captivity in terms of the predominant philosophical tendency to internalize the form of propositions as the ultimate standard for thinking about the meaningfulness of language. That is, Wittgenstein tells us that in committing ourselves to a predominant understanding of the general form of propositions, we ineluctably find ourselves bound by language. Furthermore, Wittgenstein draws the distinction between "tracing the outline of the thing's nature" and "tracing the frame through which we look at it," between the possibility of engaging what language is about and avoiding such an engagement by locking ourselves in the folds of language (entrenching ourselves in language), between a language that opens itself to the world and a language that keeps us separate from the world by trapping us within itself. Hence, according to him, if we internalize the picture that "the general form of propositions is: this is how things are," we find ourselves in a position that keeps us from genuinely responding to the thing's nature, that allows us only to reproduce the form of our reflection. When our language operates within this propositional picture, it loses (touch with) the thing whose nature it purports to delineate and thus "merely trac[es] around the frame" of the possibility of such a delineation. Or, as Wittgenstein writes a few sections earlier in the *Investigations*, "we predicate of the thing what lies in the method of representing it."[5]

But what is so problematic in the common—and commonsense—view of propositional language as a language that speaks in the form of "this is how things are"? Is this not precisely the essence of speaking—i.e., to make explicit the suchness of things? In what sense is acceptance of "the general form of propositions" indicative of an entrapment within language that cannot open up to nature? Why is the propositional a form of captivity?

The propositional entraps us when we forget its limits. It captivates us by tempting us to forget that it has limits. Thus, Wittgenstein is not only contesting a common interpretation of how to understand the particular structure of propositions, but he is, first of all, confronting the temptation of globalization. He is calling into question the philosophical conviction that the meaningfulness of language is fundamentally dependent on one general and unified form of meaning: the form of propositions. Indeed, the general form of propositions, "this is how things are," has established itself with philosophy as the fundamental form of the intelligible. I have suggested we understand this as the hegemony of the propositional.

One way to describe this hegemony is to say that the history of philosophical treatments of language has invariably regarded the propositional form of statement-making sentences as the ultimate representative of the space of language. Although philosophers prior to Wittgenstein, Heidegger, and Austin were not unaware of the variety of modes through which language makes itself available to us—the variety of ways language is there for us to make sense and non-sense, to embrace or to avoid, to question and discover, encourage and insult, dream and hope, etc.—propositional language is what has always most mattered for philosophical thought about language. While assertions and statements have been systematically made into the subject matter for inquiries into the meaning mechanisms of language, nonpropositional forms of linguistic expression are either ignored or explicitly relegated to the periphery of the philosophical concern with knowledge and truth. Hence, while we may note, for example, the exceptional interest Aristotle shows for the nonpropositional, we must also see how the gesture of exclusion by which he opens his *De Interpretatione* becomes a prototype for the manner in which philosophy sets the stage for the investigation of language:

> Every sentence is significant . . . but not every sentence is a statement-making sentence, but only those in which there is truth and falsity. There is not truth and falsity in all sentences: a prayer is a sentence but is neither true or false. The present investigation deals with the statement-making sentence; the others we can dismiss since consideration of them belongs rather to the study of rhetoric and poetry.[6]

As suggested, the twentieth-century hegemony of the propositional is probably most apparent in the Anglo-American philosophy of language governed by a conception of language in which, to use Russell's words, "the essential business of language is to assert and deny facts,"[7] what is called today "the instilling of information" or the "sharing of knowledge."[8] Language becomes, as such, the object of a philosophical discourse—part of a philosophical agenda—in which the question of meaning is essentially tied to the question of knowledge and truth. Much of the traditional philosophy of language, consequently, approaches the question of linguistic meaning exclusively in terms of the truth conditions of the sentences of a language. What sentences? Only those that can be ascribed a truth value. And so, forms of language that are not candidates for truth—i.e., nonpropositional modes of language—are regarded, to begin with, as negligible or peripheral meaning modalities. For Russell, for example, "Sentences may be interrogative, optative, exclamatory, or imperative . . . [but] we may confine ourselves to indicative sentences, since these alone are true or false."[9]

With the "pragmatic turn" in the philosophy of language, this traditional focus seems to have changed. Concern with the linguistic utterance is now seemingly inseparable from the philosophical acknowledgment of the rich field of usability, the spectrum of functionality through which language appears and participates in our lives and of which assertion is only a part. However, the opening of new domains of inquiry into the behavior of language (for instance, speech act theory) has not rid philosophy of the conception by which the core of language, or language at its core, is essentially propositional. On the contrary, the incorporation of those modalities of language that are not candidates for truth into the philosophical discussion is primarily symptomatic of the fact that the philosophy of language has totalized the rule of the propositional, that it has allowed what Brandom, for example, understands as the "pragmatic priority of the propositional" to govern the conceptualization of language as such. That is to say, the pragmatic attempt to embrace the heterogeneity of the space of language has resulted in the ultimate unification and homogenization of language's nature. The unfolding of meaning in language is thus construed on the basis of one essential modus operandi. "Language is an instrument of communication," Davidson writes, "because of its semantic dimension, the potentiality for truth or falsehood of its sentences, or better, of its utterances and inscriptions."[10] In other words, the propositional has become language's infrastructure. Propositional content is presumed to constitute the meaningfulness of language altogether, and it is thus assertive or assertorial language—the ultimate pragmatic-linguistic openness to truth—that continues to declare, "Asserting is the fundamental speech act."[11]

3. The Fact of the Propositional

The rule of the propositional in the philosophy of language is symptomatic of a deeply rooted philosophical commitment to a cognitive—or epistemic—world picture, a picture regulated by the ideal structure of cognitive judgment.[12] (Thus to object to the propositional is to object to the contention that a cognitive framework could and should ground our understanding of meaning in language.) Another way to put this is to say that the hegemony of propositions is the outcome of a basic commitment to a single homogeneous structure of intelligibility that, most clearly, finds its expression in the philosophical tendency to embrace the structure of facts as an ultimate model for the unfolding of meaning.

In this context we may understand Wittgenstein's problematization of the "general form of propositions" as resembling in its motivation Nietzsche's famous response to positivism in *The Will to Power*:

> Against positivism which halts at phenomena—"There are only *facts*"—I would say: No, facts is precisely what there is not, only interpretations.[13]

This famous passage is typically discussed in the context of nihilism or of Nietzsche's perspectivism. But, for our purposes, it also provides a succinct view of the predominant (propositional) disposition toward meaning that concerns us here (and finds its expression not only in the positivism that disturbed Nietzsche—that of Comte, Spencer, or Mill—but in a wide spectrum of philosophical positions and dispositions common to much of contemporary philosophy, and in particular the contemporary philosophy of language).[14] Positivism, according to Nietzsche, exemplifies a kind of reflective encounter with a world whose horizons are determined by one general proposition couched in a point of view that remains external to the phenomena: positivism "halts at phenomena" and states "there are only facts."

Positivism is an engagement with phenomena through the prism of facts. But, as Nietzsche's response shows us, thinking of the world in terms of facts is not, in itself, what is problematic here. Facts are common to our speech because they belong to the way we experience the world. It is a fact that she wasn't accepted to medical school, that the restaurant around the block is crowded night after night; it is a fact that two kids were killed by soldiers this morning, that a suicide bomber exploded on a downtown bus yesterday; and it is also a fact that, against all odds, the neighbour upstairs just had a baby. I don't think Nietzsche had, or should have had, any reservations about these day-to-day uses of the word. What's more, Nietzsche does not simply seek to snatch facts out of the positivist grasp, but offers an alternative (i.e., interpretations) that is not without meaning. And so, facts are not simply a target because they presuppose a perception of the world committed to the actuality and meaninfulness of things. What Nietzsche objects to, rather, is the rule or the hegemony of facts. In other words, Nietzsche is taking issue with the primary, constitutive gesture by which the positivist predetermines the frame through which the meaningfulness of the world shows itself to philosophical reflection. He counters the kind of reflection that is regulated from the beginning by a thematic generalization of the structure of the field of meaning. His critique is directed against the tendency to pro-posit, or pro-position, a uniform structure of facts as the exclusive basis for understanding the manifold, polysemantic, heterogeneous, ever-unfolding nature of phenomena.

Following Nietzsche and Wittgenstein, what concerns us here is not any specific move within a given philosophical framework as much as it is the gesture through which reflection construes the space of thinking in the first place. Positing facts, in this context, is that move which constitutes—opening up and, at the same time, leveling down—the possibility of saying whatever one has to say, whatever can be said philosophically. In particular, this is a move that eliminates from philosophy's language everything that cannot find its expression in the form of a statement.

During the twentieth century the positivistic conception of facts has been problematized and revised more than once. The philosophical thematization of facts no longer allows for a postulation of the independent status of facts vis-à-vis language or the space of the intelligible. The rhetoric concerning a rift between the world of facts and the world of thought and language has been completely rejected.[15] And, yet, something fundamental has not changed. Facts have remained the sign of a uniform monolithic structure that governs the appearance of meaning in philosophy. Looking back at a paradigmatic gesture of positing of facts, such as the one we find, for example, in Russell's *The Philosophy of Logical Atomism*, can make this clearer. Russell sets the field for his investigation in the following way:

> The first truism to which I wish to draw your attention—and I hope that you will agree with me that these things that I call truism are so obvious that it is almost laughable to mention them—is that the world contains *facts*, which are what they are whatever we may choose to think about them, and that there are also *beliefs*, which have reference to facts, and by reference to facts are either true or false.[16]

According to Russell, facts "are what they are whatever we may choose to think about them." Facts are what Nietzsche's interpretations are not. Unlike interpretations, facts "are what they are": their meaning structure is in principle self-sufficient and self-identical. In Russell's work this is indeed a claim about the autonomy of facts vis-à-vis our beliefs about them. However, Russell's phrasing contains a deeper conviction that is still shared by a great variety of contemporary philosophers who are otherwise unwilling to accept the kind of talk that presents facts and language as two distinct things. To say that "facts are what they are" is to internalize the idea that human intelligibility evolves from a unified, self-sufficient, self-identical grounding structure, that the fundamental structure of meaning is complete, objective, and essentially aperspectival. To put this another way, we may say that, in contrast to Nietzsche's interpretations, facts open themselves to (the question of) meaning only in an univocal, unilateral manner. Facts, in this context, mark a commitment to one particular mode of responsiveness, or openness, to the world. This monolithic structure is epitomized in the bifurcation of the space of thought (language) into the true and the false. The truism that the "world contains facts" functions as the infrastructure that allows and then obliges our thinking and speaking about the world to take on a truth value. That is, facts are the mark of a world that becomes meaningful primarily through the opposition between true and false, a world that, before anything else, appears as a ready-made object of judgment. Concurrently, judgment (and a judgmental or assertive relation toward the world) becomes the key to, and the constitutive principle of, any meaningful encounter we might have with the world.

The internalization of the standard of facts is, in other words, tantamount to reconstructing the intelligible on the basis of a singular commitment to one particular (i.e., cognitive) mode of openness to the world. The result is a complete homogenization of the field of meaning. That is, once the meaningfulness of language becomes ruled by the truth conditions of its sentences (truth conditions that themselves are formulated in the language of facts), meaning can never, at heart, be singular. It can never assume the form of a real event but only of a reproduced token belonging to a general, uniform apparatus. In a framework in which "all true statements have the same relation to facts,"[17] language can open up to meaning only through one uniform modus operandi: fact depiction. This means that a sentence—such as "This child is in pain"—would be paradigmatically thematized on a par with such sentences as "That bar is the standard meter stick," or "Snow is white." Homogenized in this way, language becomes a vehicle wholly indifferent to the meanings it opens and conveys. It forces us to speak of the joys of happy days or the horrors of dark days through the very same language in which I tell you what kind of milk I have in my fridge or what my phone bill was last month. Moreover, within a propositional framework, language is not only indifferent to its own meaningfulness. It is also completely detached from and remains unaffected by the persons who speak and listen to it. This is why standard conceptions of communication are based on the idea that what I say to you, you can say to me. What I mean by my words, you can mean by yours. What I understand in your speech, you can understand in mine. This symmetry, based on the indifferent uniformity of meaning, and on the mirroring of the speaking "poles," is typically understood as a prerequisite for communicability. That is, the fact that we are legible to each other is typically explained by the fact that what I mean by what I say is the same as what you mean by what you say, and that what you understand in what I say is the same as what I understand in what you say.

The alleged invariance of language in regards to its subjects, speakers, and audience is a symptom of how meanings are leveled down to modular units, which, as such, probably deserve the term typically used to designate them: *contents*. Indeed, the essential form of content, one of the most central notions in the analysis of language and meaning, is that of being contained. Content is contained meaning. It is that which is always already there, in full, wholly constituted as an object, uniform, self-sufficient, and available upon request. Content is a form of meaning whose appearance or unfolding—whose presence qua phenomenon—is rendered secondary and unessential. It is a form of meaning that, despite its embodiment in actual linguistic utterances, is never nurtured by temporality or perspective. It is, in principle, atemporal and aperspectival. And, closed as it is within the solidity of its own confines, it is completely foreign to the possibility of transcendence. Content is the prototype of self-identity, the self-identity of meaning, of meaning construed as the self-identical. Content is simply what it is: reified meaning or meaning in the form of abstract objecthood.

4. "This Is How Things Are"

The internalization of the propositional as the ultimate standard for meaning is based on the exclusion of distinctively nonpropositional forms of meaning from the heart of philosophical concern. This demarcation of a line between standard and "special" cases of speech irreversibly determines the status of distinctively nonpropositional language in a manner that poses no risk to the standard itself, having already been labeled as exceptional. Once the poetic, the metaphorical, the emotive, the nonsensical, the paradoxical, the paratactic, the wild, the untamed, the utterly uncontrollable are labeled as nonstandard or marginal cases of speech, they are unavoidably bound to serve as a constant affirmation of the uniformity of ordinary language. That is to say, once defined as the exceptional substandard of speech, these cases can only uphold the view that ordinary speech is fundamentally propositional.

Yet the exclusion of those distinctively nonpropositional cases from philosophy's consideration is, at the moment, less important for us. What concerns us, rather, is an even more crucial form of concealment by which the propositional effaces the unfolding of meaning in language. For Wittgenstein, as we've seen, the form of propositions is a binding frame that does not allow us to respond to the actual appearance of meaning. What is it then in the form of propositions that bars us from the actuality of the meaningful? If we look more closely at how Wittgenstein characterizes this general form, we notice that he is, in fact, addressing a central feature of the propositional to which we have yet given little attention. This is the thetic character of propositions manifested in the form of "this is how things are." The phrase "this is how things are" presents the essential mechanism operative in propositional language, namely, the depiction of things in an informative manner, i.e., the determination of the suchness of things in a way necessarily either true or false.

The ability of propositions to depict the way things are is dependent on a form of depiction that, on the one hand, refers to objects (allowing intended objects to come into focus and so become linguistic subjects) and, on the other hand, presents these objects through the particular prism of predicates. Propositions can present the suchness of things because the structure of the world can find expression in their method of depiction. Therefore, on a primary level, the general form "this is how things are" suits the structure of propositions that constitutes the possibility of saying something (about something)—of saying that "something is something"—of genuinely saying anything at all. In other words, the phrase "this is how things are" is indicative of what is typically perceived by the philosophical tradition to be the crux of the synthetic construction that allows words to be joined together in contentful ways.

The conviction that the appearance of meaning depends on a proper structure of articulation dates at least to the Greek understanding of logos. In Plato's *Sophist,* for instance, one of the important lessons Theaetetus learns from the Eleatic stranger is that language can only convey a logos through a particular interweaving of its elements. According to the stranger, "Words which, when spoken in succession, signify something, do fit together." However, not every succession and combination of words allow speech to convey meaning. "The signs we use in speech to signify being are surely of two kinds . . . one is called 'names,' the other 'verbs,'" and it is only when "you combine verbs with names" that language can be said to take on meaning.

> The moment you do that, they [the words] fit together and the simplest combination becomes a statement . . . now it gives information about facts or events. . . . It does not merely name something but gets you somewhere by weaving together verbs with names. Hence we say it "states" something, not merely "names" something, and in fact, it is this complex that we mean by the word "statement" (logos).[18]

According to the stranger, the appearance of a logos, or simply the possibility of saying something in a legible way (*legein*), rests on a weaving together of two different kinds of linguistic elements. Without a proper linguistic weaving of these elements, the textility of language cannot contain the texture of things. But though responsible for making the presentation of meaning possible, this synthesis actually recedes into the background of what is said. And the only trace it leaves of itself is the auxiliary verb *is*: Something is Something, the subject of the sentence is what the sentence says (predicates) it is—x is P.

As we know, and as is so clearly apparent in the above translation of the passage from Plato, the inherited form connecting a sentence's subject and predicate—"x is P"—is paradigmatically identified with the form of statements or propositions. The philosophical tradition typically renders these two forms as essentially interchangeable: statements assume the form of "x is P" (to state something is to state that "x is P"); and what is stated in "x is P" is the fact that x is P, namely, that this is how things are. And yet, the traditional congruence between the articulative structure underlying an indicative sentence (x is P) and the propositional form should not be taken for granted. The possibility of this congruence is not the result of an innocuous philosophical reading, but, as Heidegger shows, of a reductive appropriation of the question of meaning symptomatic of what, in his view, is the tradition's abandonment of the original—Greek—sense of logos. For Heidegger, more specifically, the reduction of logos to the structure of statements (of discourse, *Rede,* to assertion, *Aussage*) is indicative of how philosophical reflection remains trapped within the confines of "the ontology of the present-at-hand" and of how, being governed by the concept of cognitive judgement, it systematically covers up the origins of human meaningfulness.

This paradigmatic tendency to assimilate the presentation of "something as something" under the general form of propositions is, I take it, also the target of Wittgenstein's criticism against the manner in which the form "this is how things are" prevents us from hearing the actual speaking—the nature—of the things presented in language. Propositions force a deafness on us. They lock us in the house of language and permit us to engage with nature only by looking at it through language's sealed windows. Wittgenstein, however, does not tell us much about the possibility of an alternative. This is a general feature of his writing. While his descriptions of our captivity in language are generally elaborate and nuanced, the experience of freedom in language is only rarely hinted at by him. At the same time, however, it seems clear from the above passage that, if it were possible to encounter the nature of things in language, then this possibility must be grounded in a relation to language that does not subject the suchness of things to the form of propositions.

The point is this: our life with language allows us to speak of the way things are without necessarily committing our speech to the form of propositional representations. What the rule of the propositional hides, in other words, is not only the distinctively nondescriptive areas of language that it relegates to the periphery of the meaningful. More important, it is the very nature of our speaking about the suchness of things, the actual character of the human possibility of allowing the textility of language to contain, as Plato has it, the texture of things. The secret hidden by the propositional is that it is itself secondary to and derivative from the manner in which language's "weaving together" of "x as P" originally opens to meaning. The propositional conceals the primacy of "x is P." It conceals a difference, an invisible difference whose presence explains why when we say such daily things as "It's raining again," "I miss you," "Dinner is ready," "You are beautiful" we are usually not at all saying that "this is how things are."

5. The Bell Jar

In the following chapters I shall try to elaborate further the sense in which the propositional covers up the appearance of meaning in language. This will be done because the search for the personal coincides with the attempt to recover dimensions of the experience of meaning the propositional completely levels. At this point, however, it should be enough to develop some sense of the suppressive character of the propositional by noticing the irreducible presence of a difference that exists between the presentation of—a language that presents—x as P and the proposition *that* x is P. This difference is evasive. And upon reflection its evasiveness becomes even more tricky because reflection itself is quite biased on this point: it does not seem to allow us to speak legibly about the *such*ness of things unless we also admit that what we say is that "this is how things are." For example, I cannot, or so it seems, say anything such as "I am thirty-nine years old" without admitting to the fact that what I said is that I am thirty-nine years old—that this is indeed my age, that this is how things are. Even if I were to have, for a passing moment, some hesitation or reluctance in affirming this identity, reflection has its ways of putting you in your place: Were you, in saying "I am thirty-nine years old," not stating that this is how things are, that it is true you are thirty-nine, that it is the case that you are about to turn forty? You clearly were not saying anything else, anything different, were you?

Still, why don't I feel comfortable with the place in which reflection puts me? What would it mean to release the intelligibility of language from the binding grip of the propositional? I think that an important step can be taken here once we recognize the following distinctive feature so characteristic of the workings of propositions: the propositional not only conveys how things are, but, more important, establishes that this is how they are—it ascertains that things are the way they are. Propositions not only present meaning but, more important, also package what they present and present what they package. They not only enable the meaningfulness of the indicative "x is P" to show itself, but do so by appropriating the possibility of seeing x as P in a particular, determinative manner. How? Again, by stating *that* . . . (x is P). By construing meaning in the form of the stated. Propositions posit, position (or even *proposition*) meaning. They articulate the intelligible by making meaning stand erect. This is the true significance of their thetic structure. Erection is the general form of propositions.

This can be said another way: the distinctive meaningfulness of the propositional is based on a built-in structure of reflexivity that produces and, at the same time, closes on and frames its own presentations. The propositional is a frame, one that can allegedly frame just about everything, including itself. And this is because "there are only facts," because the suchness dictated by facts allows for no meaning that is not essentially framable. Moreover, propositional meaning not only rests on how language relates to (represents, depicts, makes explicit) the order of the factical. This meaning is itself always already subordinate to that order. In a propositional world meaning itself is (regarded as) a kind of fact. This fact is, in principle, always representable and reproducible. It can always be framed again and again, always reformed into yet another kind of fact—the cat is on the mat (to use one of the most familiar philosophical examples): it is a fact that the cat is on the mat, X stated that the cat is on the mat (it is a fact that he stated that . . .), Y believes that X stated that the cat is on the mat, she informs Z that she heard that X stated that . . . Thus, an infinite reproduction of ever new meanings is generated that, in a deeper sense, are not new at all because they can never transcend the given order of the factual, never open up beyond the uniform and structurally predetermined standards of the propositional.

So, to conclude this chapter, what is it exactly that the propositional hides from us?

Since propositional language can state anything whatsoever, we may say that, in an obvious sense, it hides nothing from us. The form of propositions is the unbounded frame of a window through which everything, in principle, can become part of our view: the sky and the moon and the sea; the cities, the streets, the houses, the people, deeds, emotions, etc. Nothing whatsoever escapes the view that the propositional window opens for us. However, this window has one peculiar feature we need to note: while allowing for an unbounded view of the phenomena, the window can never open. No air can come in through this window, and there is no way to stretch out your hand and collect the drops of the first rain. God allowed Moses to see the promised land on the condition that he did not enter it. The propositional too allows us to face the phenomena—as Nietzsche's positivist does—but since it gives us the phenomena only in the form of that which we face from a distance, it consequently transforms the real into the virtual. Propositional language is virtual language. It is the virtual double of the actual appearance of the meaningful. Moreover, it is an assertive kind of double that insists we forget what the actual unfolding of meaning is like. The propositional frames for us every possible aspect of the meaningful, but always leaves us on the other side of the sealed window frame. It gives us everything at the cost of our freedom. It locks us in that stifling domain of virtual possibilities that Sylvia Plath, for example, termed the "bell jar." Yet, due to the transparency of the bell jar, we are so often tempted to forget our captivity, to forget that the possibility exists for us to return, as Husserl puts it, to the things themselves.

CHAPTER 2
The Limits of Language and the Dream of Transcendence

1. Philosophy and Disappointment

What philosophers say about reality is often as disappointing as a sign you see in a shop window, which reads: Pressing Done Here. If you brought your clothes to be pressed, you would be fooled; for the sign is for sale.[1]

In this aphorism appearing in "Diapsalmata," the opening section of *Either/Or*, Kierkegaard is concerned with a disappointment, a disappointment that awaits the individual—addressed here as "you"—who follows philosophy and internalizes its perspective. Philosophy, according to Kierkegaard, is bound to disappoint you. Is this a complaint? Is it a warning? A prognosis? Is disappointment an unavoidable consequence of the engagement with philosophy and, as such, is it an essential predicament of philosophy? More to the point, what exactly is disappointing about philosophy? What kind of disappointment is Kierkegaard speaking of in this aphorism?

The relationship between an individual's disappointment and the misleading, even deceptive, character of philosophy is at the center of our attention here. The basic outline of the analogy seems quite explicit: the sign in the shop window relates to the inside of the shop as philosophy (or philosophers) relate to reality. Consequently, just as the sign in the window fools the individual who takes it seriously, philosophy seems to mislead the individual. This happens on at least two levels. First, there is an inadequate representation of reality, of what the facts are inside the shop. And, in this failure to adequately represent reality, philosophy then fails to practically instruct the individual and guide her or his everyday conduct. In other words, on a first reading of this aphorism, philosophy appears to be a dubious enterprise not only because of the manner in which it misleads you about the nature of reality but also because of the manner in which it distracts you from realizing your human needs, subsequently preventing the individual from leading (what could be understood as) a happy, or good, life. Putting this more directly, we can say that philosophy disappoints the individual on both an epistemological and an ethical level, and that the latter disappointment is made even more problematic by the disparaging suggestion that the language of philosophy (the sign) is for sale.

Upon a closer look, however, we may note that Kierkegaard is not actually concerned with the content of any specific philosophical thesis expounded by this or that philosopher. The problem with "what philosophers say about reality" does not simply issue from the production of false representations. Kierkegaard's analogy, rather, shows that the disappointment created by philosophy results from the character and form of its language. More specifically, philosophy is presented as disappointing not because of its failure to adequately represent, but because of its inability to represent at all. Just as the sign's only reference is self-reference—its form of representation being self-presentation—the language of philosophy is not misleading because of any false content, but because of its false appearance as contentful.

This leads us to a reformulation of Kierkegaard's complaint. In philosophy, we may now claim, language has a form that cannot in principle make room for the possibility of truth. Philosophy is not simply wrong or untrue; it is entirely outside the kind of relation to reality that allows for opening the question of truth (or falsehood) in the first place. Philosophy, according to Kierkegaard, suffers from a structural failure inherent in its very language and thought. This structural condition prevents philosophy from engaging those dimensions of reality that matter to the individual. In other words, philosophy's modus operandi is based on a misplacement of those very areas of meaning that are most crucial to the individual.

This brings us to a central and recurring theme in Kierkegaard's work: a critique of the manner in which the language of philosophy elides the question of human existence. Kierkegaard's work provides a reflexive philosophical prototype for contesting the effacement of the individual by philosophy's own language. And this is also how it becomes so relevant to our investigation of the personal. For Kierkegaard, "the difficulty that inheres in existence, with which the existing individual is confronted, is one that never really comes to expression in the language of abstract thought."[2] According to him, the meaningfulness of individual existence not only presents itself as philosophy's most crucial question but also brings philosophy into a critical confrontation with its greatest limitation. Existence is precisely what abstract thought cannot think, what theoretical language cannot express, and, thus, what systematic philosophy cannot encounter. If we recall the terms used in the previous chapter, we may say that the language of thought holds us captive and that, according to Kierkegaard, our captivity in the "language of abstract thought" keeps us from encountering the existence of the individual or, better, keeps individuality from showing itself.[3]

Why is this so? What exactly is the relationship between the structure of abstract language and the inability to make a place in language for the individual? What is the nature of the gap between existence and abstract intelligibility? What is in the structure of abstract language that obliterates the singularity of personal existence? Although Kierkegaard does not propose a unified answer to these questions, two constitutive features of abstract language stand out as central: these are generality and possibility. For Kierkegaard, abstract language is bound to efface the singularity of existence because its structure is essentially general (or universal). And it cannot make room for the actuality of existence because it operates and is grounded in the sphere of the possible.

2. Language: The Map

In *Concluding Unscientific Postscript* Kierkegaard articulates these aspects of abstractness with the following image:

> To exist under the guidance of pure thought is like travelling in Denmark with the help of a small map of Europe on which Denmark shows no larger than a steel pen-point, aye, it is still more impossible.[4]

When discussing the individuality of the individual, the language of thought is like a useless map. As in the case of the window sign, Kierkegaard again draws an analogy between philosophy and a form of representation designed to serve the needs of the individual, but failing to do so in principle. Moreover, like the window sign, the map is a representation that is not, in itself, incorrect or inaccurate. It is simply ineffectual in the context relevant to the individual. The map represents reality in a manner so general that it does not allow the individual to find his place or further direct himself. We can say that the map's mode of representation—its structure—presents reality in a way that unavoidably fails to make room for the concrete individual and the singularity of his idiosyncratic domain of deliberation and action. Although the map represents reality in a manner that would seem to include the location of the individual, the generality of this representation assimilates the place of the individual, depriving the place of its particularity. An individual who uses the map is provided with general knowledge concerning his location. He may know, for example, the distance between the different European capitals. He can also correctly identify that point on the map that represents his relative position (e.g., Denmark). But the traveler cannot orient his specific journey on the map because it contains no trace of the road he has been traveling. Analogically, since generality is the basis of the representational character of language—since the basic units of linguistic representation are types, or generic categories, that are not in themselves tied to the specificity of that which they are about—the individual cannot find within language the means for coming to terms with his singularity.

But the analogy between the map and the language of abstract thought has another important aspect. The "small map of Europe" is not only an image of a representation whose generality cannot contain the singularity of the individual's location; it is also an example of a mode of representation that essentially remains external to that which it represents. The map is an apposite image for Kierkegaard because it exemplifies a form of representation that, like abstract language, is not grounded in the actual domain it represents but is, rather, always located at some indefinite point outside of it. More specifically, the map's mechanism of representation is one that is based on the generalization of all possible perspectives into an ideal, totally external point of view. The map represents reality from an ideally constructed point of view. The representation it provides is thus aperspectival. What grounds the map's representation is the projection of an ideal perspective from which all represented points appear to be equally close or distant. (Upon looking at a modern map your home appears just as close, or distant—in effect, distantless—as that place on the other side of the world that appears in your dreams but to which you have never ventured.) The map, in other words, opens up the meaningfulness of what it represents by altogether obliterating the presence of distance and by completely homogenizing the appearance of meaning: the map is comprised of a set of objective (objectified) points that all have exactly the same status and significance and that all open up in exactly the same way to anyone, anywhere, who looks at them. In this respect the map is not only an ideal construction, but a construction of meaning that internalizes the anonymous gaze of everyone as its standard.

Abstract language construes the realm of meaning on the basis of the possible rather than the actual. Consequently, the very gesture of speaking about the existence of the individual is bound by a structure that not only excludes existence from the domain of the intelligible but also leaves no trace of this very exclusion. According to Kierkegaard, "existence constitutes the highest interest of the existing individual and his interest in his existence constitutes his reality." Yet, "what reality is cannot be expressed in the language of abstraction" because abstract thought operates as a "medium within which the concept [of reality] is thought not in reality but in possibility." That is, "all that is said about reality is really said within the sphere of the possible."⁵

To explain this further, let us recall our discussion, in the previous chapter, of the aperspectival essence—that self-contained core—of propositional language. The underlying presupposition of propositional language is that its basis of articulation—the locus of meaning—is always already "there" in the form of the factual. It is there as a fully constituted, self-sufficient objecthood whose different aspects can be framed or captured by the statements of our language. Furthermore, the general form of propositions only allows meaning to appear on the condition that it remains fully subordinate to, and regulated by, the ideal of an all-encompassing, general, and homogeneous order of intelligibility. Under such a condition, the meaningfulness of the individual can only assume a derivative form: the possibility of saying anything—of saying something—about the individual is derived from more fundamental meaning structures, i.e., from facts that, as Russell puts it, simply "are what they are." Whatever can be said propositionally about an individual or by an individual must, thus, take the form of an utterance, deriving its meaning from a constellation of facts. Within the horizons of this language of facts there is no place for the individual to become meaningful in any primary or fundamental manner, that is, in a manner that respects the primacy of her individuality. Accordingly, when I speak of myself, or of my relation to you, I am paradigmatically taken to be speaking of the factual constellation to which you and I belong. From a propositional perspective, I seem to be speaking of a factual configuration whose form of meaningfulness is essentially prior to and independent of the concreteteness of the singular individual who is the ostensible subject of the utterance. To put this differently, the singularity of the individual cannot belong to the pulsing heart of language because the structure of propositions anchors the possibility of meaningfulness and understanding in an objective world of facts. The structure of propositions presupposes a monolithically self-sufficient, atemporal, and aperspectival constellation in which there can be no room for, and no trace of, what cannot be derived from the intelligibility of the factual. This is precisely what Nietzsche's positivist says: "There are only facts."

Hence, in saying, for example, that you miss her or that that you have been thinking a lot about her lately, your language may indeed depict your relation with her. However, as long as this remains within the parameters of the propositional, it is neither your individuality nor hers (not your existence as individuals) that seem to be in any way crucial to the meaningfulness of what you say. On the contrary, the meaningfulness of your words seems to be grounded in a fact structure that bestows meaning regardless of who you are, without any particular connection to your particular existence. The gravitational center of your words is constituted by the fact that a certain person has been thinking about another lately. This person happens to be you, but the singularity of your being remains completely external to the meaning of your words.

In other words, the intelligibility of your statement does not, so it seems, originate from the concrete particularity of your situation but from the abstract possibility of one person missing, or thinking a lot about, another person. In the same fashion, it seems that I can understand what you say about your feelings toward her (only) because I understand the concept of "missing someone" and because I can apply my understanding of this general possibility to your situation. That is, your words express the fact that you are in the position of someone who misses, or who thinks a lot about, someone else. In this respect, speaking about yourself is essentially the same as speaking (or thinking) about anyone who can be in your position. The language of propositions renders you identical to anyone who might be in your shoes.

One can say that, when the propositional sets the grounds for our speech, information becomes the essence of language. Yet a language whose essence is "instilling information,"[6] as McDowell insists, is a language indifferent to whom one speaks of, to whom one listens. Information is a form of intelligibility that excludes us as individuals. That is to say, the language of information is a language in which our individuality is ultimately irrelevant. If, in speaking to me, information is all you wish to hear in my language, then I am not relevant to you as the individual I am.

With Kierkegaard we see how the form of conceptual or (propositional) content determines a standard of intelligibility that does not allow the spoken to embrace the singularity of the self in any genuine manner. His diagnosis of the manner in which the individual is lost in abstract language thus serves as a starting point for the present investigation. At the same time, however, we also need to notice that the strong and direct connection Kierkegaard draws between the elision of the individual and the hegemony of the propositional is symptomatic not only of philosophical language but everyday language as well. Thus, as we explore the sense in which existence is obscured by the sphere of the possible, we discover that the objective linguistic structure problematized by Kierkegaard is not only a part of philosophical discourse but is characteristic of our most ordinary linguistic routines.

According to Kierkegaard, language's inability to encounter and embrace existence is not only a philosophical or theoretical failure. It is a much more deeply situated human predicament, for the singular meaning of individual existence is necessarily obliterated within the very bounds of everyday intelligibility. In ordinary life the possibility of being meaningful precludes the possibility of being a genuine individual. This is one possible formulation—a language or linguistically oriented formulation—of what Kierkegaard understands to be the problem of authenticity. Specifically, as we become who we are as persons, meaningful in a variety of ways, our individuation never seems to be singular. It is always already dependent on, and subordinate to, a public condition of meaningfulness that we can only internalize but never constitute, let alone establish an alternative form of intelligibility to. We, as persons, are in the deepest sense of the word neither the source nor the masters of the means by which we become meaningful. This is because our individuation must emanate from forms of meaning already present in the public sphere of possibilities, and the limits of this sphere are the limits of intelligibility as such. If we thus adopt the primary sense of the word *authentic*, we may conclude that the possibility of being your own self is, in principle, nonlocatable within this horizon of meaning.

The problem of authenticity surfaces in response to the apparent difficulty, perhaps the impossibility, of becoming meaningful in the face of a precondition of meaning essentially external and general, one indifferent to and detached from your singular being. What gives rise to this question of authenticity is exactly that recognition of the structure of the intelligible as being in conflict with (the possibility of ascribing meaning to) genuine individuality. Recognizing the ineluctability of this structural condition, Kierkegaard nevertheless refuses to embrace it. As such, he calls for resisting that which he considers to be unavoidable.

A philosopher's response to "the necessary" (be it logical and/or factual) is never just a move within a given philosophical framework. It is, rather, indicative of deep philosophical and even prephilosophical dispositions upon which philosophical frameworks rely and that serve as the source of fundamental philosophical divides. In particular, the divide between twentieth-century Continental thought, on the one hand, and analytic or Anglo-American philosophy, on the other, can be understood through the differences between these two schools over the relationship between logical necessity and the question of truth. In Kierkegaard, however, the constraints of the intelligible (which appear as the limits of language) are both recognized and accepted while also being questioned and challenged. What is at stake for Kierkegaard is the very possibility of the individual suspending the structure of generality intrinsic to the phenomenon of meaning. This question can also be asked in terms of the relation between existence and facts. Given that human intelligibility is indeed grounded in the factual, does the language of facts really exhaust the meaning of the individual? Or, in contrast, can we meaningfully speak of the individual, or of the meaningfulness of the individual, without submitting our speech to the reign of the factual? These questions ultimately open up for Kierkegaard a paradox: the "paradox that the single individual is higher than the universal" or that "there is an interiority that is incommensurable with exteriority."[7] I shall not explicate the Kierkegaardian notion of this paradox and its ramifications in the aesthetic, the ethical, and the religious spheres of existence. But since I do wish to provide a sense of how Kierkegaard raises the very paradoxicality of individual meaning, I shall focus on a figure central to his discussion, that of Abraham.

3. Language and Silence: The Example of Abraham

In *Fear and Trembling* Kierkegaard approaches the problem of individuality in a figurative manner. This should not be surprising. Kierkegaard wants to avoid an abstract treatment of the possibility of authenticity, since a language that posits—a propositional language—will not then be able to allow for the disclosure that he seeks. And so, instead of saying what authenticity is, Kierkegaard attempts a showing of it. He does this by turning to a central figure in the Judaic-Christian imagination. Given Kierkegaard's concern with the exemplification of a radical form of individuality, this may seem, at first, to be a peculiar turn. Yet, contrary to what we might expect, Kierkegaard is not concerned with the aberrant, the marginal, or the anomalous that typically represent an opposition to communal consensus. Instead, he focuses on a figure whose story has been completely subsumed by a tradition that, in turn, has made Abraham an exemplary hero.

Kierkegaard sees in the renowned story of Abraham an opportunity to subvert the traditional perception of individuality and faith. He seeks in particular to break from the common understanding of the source of Abraham's greatness, namely, "that he loved God in such a way that he was willing to offer him the best" (28). The crux of Abraham's story for Kierkegaard does not lie in Abraham's offer to God of something dear to him, but in the situation in which Abraham finds himself: having to intentionally carry out a difficult, horrifying decision that is, in principle, unjustifiable and even illegible. Kierkegaard is less concerned with either Abraham's total sacrifice or his absolute obedience to God than with his conscious decision to murder his beloved son.

Several aspects of Abraham's decision should be addressed. First, Abraham not only sacrifices a specific object of love within his world, but sacrifices the very form of that world. Isaac is not a simple object of Abraham's love. He is the actual center of gravity around which Abraham's life is organized. Isaac is the fulfillment of Abraham's and Sarah's hopes for a child (and in this sense the justification of many long years of suffering). He is the source of joy in their old age and holds the promise of a blessed future extending beyond them. In giving up Isaac, thus, Abraham is called upon to revoke the form that holds the story of his life together. Furthermore, the call, or decision, to kill Isaac necessarily implies Abraham's radical rejection of the fundamental ethical value of human life. In taking the life of one who has done him no harm, Abraham finds himself in the paradoxical position of intentionally acting against his most basic beliefs: breaking the primordial commitment that accords his life its human and social form. Indeed, Abraham's task is even more terrible since he intends to kill a person—a child—who is not only innocent and helpless but, moreover, trusting and entirely dependent on him. In other words, in addition to committing a murder, Abraham is a father who decides to break his paternal commitment to his son, who chooses to betray his son.

By emphasizing these aspects of Abraham's story, Kierkegaard opens up the possibility of a different reading. In this alternative reading Abraham exemplifies the possibility of a meaningful existence whose significance cannot be captured in terms of the language of thought. Abraham, in his turn against the human and the communal foundations of his existence, exemplifies a contradiction whose presence is meaningful even though it makes no sense. We can say that Abraham exemplifies the possibility of a meaningfulness that resists explanation. Abraham, according to Kierkegaard, takes a radical course of action whose meaning, constituted as it is by an internal contradiction, escapes understanding. He is about to destroy what he loves and cares about and is committed to but is motivated neither by a practical aim nor a psychological need. Abraham is a person whose deeds cannot be mapped onto a rational matrix of reasons, causes, and justifications, neither psychological, pragmatic, ideological, or any other.

Kierkegaard's Abraham is an example of a person who undertakes an act that is meaningful in a manner transcending language. That is to say, the manner in which Abraham differs from what can be said about him is not factual. The meaning of his act cannot be expressed in language because language generates forms of meaning that are, in principle, dependent on the structure of facts. More specifically, although Abraham is no murderer, the facts of the matter do not distinguish him from one. Nothing makes Abraham different from a murderer. But we may also say that what makes Abraham different from a murderer is nothing, and that this nothing is precisely where we should look for individual existence. (This is what Heidegger does, for example, in "What is Metaphysics.") Existence is located in a lacuna that, in the space of language, appears in the form of a nothing.

Unable to communicate the significance of his action, Abraham finds himself in the position of "an emigrant from the sphere of the universal" (115) Language is at his service, as usual, but he can no longer make use of it since its structure precludes the possibility of saying the one thing that really matters to him. In this sense, "Abraham *cannot* speak." And because "he cannot say that which would explain everything (that is, so that it is understandable; 115),"Abraham turns to silence.

> Abraham remains silent—but he cannot speak. Therein lies the distress and anxiety. Even though I go on day and night without interruption, if I cannot make myself understood when I speak, then I am not speaking. This is the case with Abraham. He can say everything, but one thing he cannot say, and if he cannot say that—that is, say it in such a way that the other understands it—then he is not speaking. The relief provided by speaking is that it translates me into the universal. *(113)*

For Kierkegaard, Abraham's silence manifests a singular disposition toward his exile from the sphere of the intelligible. Abraham is a person who experiences and understands the impossibility of translating his existence into language. For him, silence is the only way of embracing the paradox of his individual existence: silence is a sign of his intimate knowledge of both the limits of language and the dimensions of meaning that language cannot embrace.

> As explained above, the distress and anxiety in the paradox were due in particular to the silence: Abraham cannot speak, unless one wishes him out of the paradox again, so that he suspends it in the decisive moment and thereby ceases to be Abraham and nullifies all that preceded. *(118)*

Abraham's silence is a response to—a choice made in the face of—the bounds of the intelligible. But there can be other kinds of response. In his writing, and particularly in his telling the story of Abraham's silence, Kierkegaard himself pursues a different route from that of his protagonist. Kierkegaard, a prolific writer, chooses to contest the bounds of language while remaining within language. Kierkegaard speaks, and the pseudonym he adopts for narrating the story of Abraham, Johannes de Silentio, already reveals the affinity between his own writing and Abraham's silence. Johannes de Silentio, the author of *Fear and Trembling*, clearly operates within the realm of language. At the same time, as his name indicates, he comes to language—or language comes to him—from silence. De Silentio is a writer who claims to resist the paradigmatic—the propositional—foundations of intelligibility by embracing silence as the inner form of his language, that is, by attuning his language not to facts but to that which can only register as nothing.

4. The Limits of Language and the Question of Freedom

What exactly does it mean to enable language to reverberate nothing? Is de Silentio the name, the mark, of a philosophical attempt and, perhaps, a philosophical possibility analogous to the path inscribed in the poetry of Czeslaw Milosz: "I speak to you with silence like a cloud or a tree"?[8] For Kierkegaard, the question of writing is tied to his conception of "indirect communication." Yet, without opening this complex interpretive issue, we may already identify that feature of Kierkegaard's language most pertinent to our discussion: the paradox. The paradox marks Kierkegaard's insistence on creating a place for that which, in principle, cannot be integrated into, and even threatens the cohesiveness of, the propositional framework. While functioning within the propositional limits of intelligibility—he accepts the inevitability of these limitations—Kierkegaard contests the hegemony of the propositional by making the structure of paradox the gravitational center of his language.

In many respects, this is also how Wittgenstein reads Kierkegaard, which is particularly interesting in the context of our discussion. Explaining in conversations with the Vienna Circle "what Heidegger means by Being and Dread," Wittgenstein points to Kierkegaard as an example of a thinker who, like himself and Heidegger, recognizes man's "impulse to run up against the limits of language." According to Wittgenstein, "this running up against, Kierkegaard also recognized and even designated it in a quite similar way (as running up against paradox)."9

For Wittgenstein, the appearance of a paradox in Kierkegaard should be read as a manifestation of the latter's uncompromising, or perhaps ironic, struggle against the limitations constituting language as such. Thinking of our "language condition" as a form of captivity implies an understanding, often accompanied by a distinctive experience, of language as a limit. Philosophy is not unfamiliar with the sort of moments in which its own language seems to become a limitation, moments in which philosophy finds itself (throughout its history) face to face with dimensions of meaning—the transcendent, the mystical, the ineffable, etc.—that it could not integrate (in any straightforward manner) into its language. These are spheres of meaning that the structure of philosophical language, or of language in general, seems unable to reflect. Once recognizing the limits and limitations of language (that philosophy has also occasionally denied), the traditional patterns of response range from accepting the limiting structure of language (e.g., by keeping silent about that which cannot be said), transcending these limits by abandoning language altogether (which leads, again, to certain types of silence), and struggling against, or subverting, the established order of intelligibility imposed by language (through poetry, nonsense, paradox). What these forms of response share, despite their differences—again applying in different ways to both Kierkegaard and at least the early Wittgenstein—is the assumption that what can be expressed and heard in ordinary language is necessarily bound by language's structural limitations. This is to say that language, because of its structural limitations, imposes an impassable boundary, a horizon beyond which the meaningfulness of what we say cannot find expression. Philosophical responses to this problem of language's limits typically thematize language's limits as a necessary form of captivity. That is, the philosophical reflection on the limits of language is typically governed by the opposition between structure and freedom.

But this is a misleading opposition. It is particularly misleading when trying to think about the structure of the propositional and the ostensible impossibility in hearing, or opening up to, the personal. And so, while the structure of language can indeed be said to bar us from the personal, we need also to remember that language is the very place where the personal shows itself. Language is the form that conceals the personal, but it is also through language that the personal resonates. The personal belongs to what we say between us. Thus, the attempt to uncover the personal does not depend on transgressing the boundaries of philosophical or everyday language. Neither going beyond language nor "running up against the limits of language" will open up for us the possibility of encountering the personal. What we need, rather, is to learn to listen, to become open and responsive to the ways—evasive at times—in which the personal (the individual, the singular, the idiosyncratic) is always already lodged within language, embodied in its unfolding.

As such, our concern here is a philosophical disclosure that develops in a twofold manner. On the one hand, we must recognize how our captivation by the propositional picture, by the "general form of propositions," keeps us from responding to the personal. On the other hand, however, we must not allow this very recognition of our captivity by the propositional to become, in itself, a form of captivity. In order to uncover the personal, it is not enough to see—as Kierkegaard, for example, does—the delimiting effect of language's structure, to see how the propositional form levels individuality. It is also important to free ourselves from the (commonly tempting) position that totalizes the effect of language's limits and perceives the structural limitations of language as all encompassing.

Think again of Wittgenstein's fly caught in the bottle. There is no question that the fly is trapped and that its entrapment is a function of the constraints imposed by the particular structure of the bottle. At the same time, it is also evident that the fly's captivity is perpetuated by its misunderstanding of the form of this captivity, by a fixation that diverts the fly from perceiving the exit and that leads it, instead, to insist on "running up against . . . the limits." The way out of the bottle is never actually out of the fly's reach. But its possibility of freedom can only open up—the way out of the bottle can only show itself—when the fly relinquishes the project of overcoming or transgressing its structural limits. This will happen only when the fly abandons the point of view by which its freedom and its captivity appear as mutually exclusive. This is also where the analogy ends. A fly's world is, and should remain, too narrow to explain the kind of change that concerns us here: one based not only on the possibility of loosening the grip that the limits of language have on us but, perhaps more important, of taking (up) new forms of responsibility toward our language and its limits. (There is, indeed, something basically unsatisfying in Wittgenstein's treatment of the theme of freedom).

The same perspective that allows us to see the limits of language may tempt us to internalize these limits as constitutive in themselves of the border between language's "inside" and its unspoken "outside," a border that determines what can and cannot appear in language, what belongs and what cannot belong to the domain of shared intelligibility. In emphasizing the significance of structure, that is, we may be prone to forget that the question of freedom—our freedom—in language remains completely open for us. The fact that language has structural limitations—and doesn't structure always imply limitations?—does not absolve us from searching for this freedom. We must recognize that, in spite of the hegemony of propositional structure, we are still free not to relegate the singularity of the speaking individual outside of language. Furthermore, it is our responsibilty to search for a mode of being or a form of orientation—to develop an ear—that will allow us to hear the personal despite the limits imposed by the propositional.

Such a search begins, as suggested, in recognizing that the propositional and the personal are not mutually exclusive, that the appearance and the concealment of the personal are not opposites. Language tends to obscure the personal. But it does not, and as long as language remains human it cannot, nullify its presence. Language conceals the personal, but it is precisely in this concealment that language also embodies the personal. That is to say, the form of concealment is the personal's form of appearance. This means that we should resist the common images by which we think of concealment. If language conceals the personal, it does not do so as a veil shrouds a sacred statue, or a mask hides a face, or a hand closes on a pebble, or the earth holds within itself a long forgotten treasure.

The personal is hidden within language in the same way that beauty or emotion may hide in your face. How could I have missed it before? Take, for instance, that conversation I had with S. Facing each other, sitting on uncomfortable chairs in her studio, she speaks of her dead father. Each time she mentions him—by name or just by reference to "my dad"—her face twists into a wide, unfamiliar, artificial smile. At first, I do not understand it. As time passes, however, it dawns on me that S. is not smiling at all. In fact, she is crying. What I see—that which I see—is her in her crying.

The analogy to discovering a hidden image in a painting may also be appropriate. Think, for example, of the experience of finally seeing "something new" hidden in that oblong figure whose intriguing (or unsettling) presence dominates Holbein's double portrait, *The Ambassadors*. Think of how the authority of the eye is contested when we realize that the serene, intricate matrix of masterfully detailed objects envelopes within itself the subversive image of a skull; of how Holbein's perspectival technique of anamorphosis allows a given visual image to escape legibility when viewed from an ordinary perspective while, at the same time, enabling an illegible image to assume full coherence when viewed from an unconventional point of view.[10] Anamorphosis is a visual cryptogram. But its mechanism of concealment is not based on the suspension of some inaccessible depth of the visual field. What is hidden in the painting is found on the painting's surface and should not be sought beyond it. That is, there is nothing in the painting's actual appearance that bars us from seeing what we do not see. Our inability to apprehend the painting's hidden dimension stems, rather, from the manner in which we habitually position ourselves when regarding a painting. Our sightlessness is the result of our fixation on, our tendency to take for granted, a particular perspective from which we expect the painting to show itself to us. Likewise, the personal elides us and will continue to do so as a result of our common tendency to engage or listen to language in a manner that renders the question of freedom irrelevant. And so, just as the first step in accessing the hiddenness of an anamorphic composition entails releasing ourselves from the hegemonic perspective that frames our viewing (and constitutes the so-called limits of the picture), the turn toward the personal in language should begin by calling into question not only the hegemony of the propositional structure but also the view that accepts, and internalizes, the limits of language—as if they were given independently of our relation to the way we situate ourselves in language, independently of our being in language.

5. Before the Law of Language

We cannot hope to understand the personal if we allow the limits of language to exclude us from the question of our freedom. This is what happens, for example, to the "man from the country" described by Kafka in "Before the Law." Let us take a short look at the circumstances of this story. The man from the country seeks to be admitted to the Law, but the doorkeeper, standing before the Law, insists that he cannot grant him admittance.

> The man thinks it over and then asks if he will be allowed in later. "It is possible," says the doorkeeper "but not at the moment." Since the gate stands open as usual, and the doorkeeper steps to one side, the man stoops to peer through the gateway into the interior. Observing that, the doorkeeper laughs and says: "if you are so drawn to it, just try to go in despite my veto. But take note: I am powerful. And I am only the least of the doorkeepers. From hall to hall there is one doorkeeper after another, each more powerful than the last. The third doorkeeper is already so terrible that even I cannot bear to look at him." These are difficulties the man from the country has not expected; the Law, he thinks, should surely be accessible at all times and to everyone, but as he now takes a closer look at the doorkeeper ... he decides that it is better to wait until he gets permission to enter.

The doorkeeper gives him a stool and lets him sit down at one side of the door. There he sits for days and years.[11]

What concerns us here is the man's relationship to language, to the language of the doorkeeper, who is the representative of the Law. How does the man from the country relate to the doorkeeper's language? He takes for granted that the doorkeeper's language is a language of facts, a language whose "essential business," to use Russell's phrase, "is to assert and deny facts."[12]

Perceiving the speech of the doorkeeper as propositional, the man from the country bars himself from seeing the pragmatic force of the doorkeeper's prohibition. He internalizes the latter's veto as if it were a direct statement of fact, a clear and definitive manifestation of the impossibility of entrance into the Law. The man from the country is, of course, not happy with this fact, and he even attempts to dispute it. But he disputes it while accepting the stated fact as, in itself, definitive. In other words, he accepts the language of the doorkeeper as a necessity and a limit, in itself absolute and unquestionable.

The man from the country ends up spending his whole lifetime at the gate of the Law. During the years he spends at the gate, he seeks to contest again and again the limits posed by the doorkeeper. "He makes many attempts to be admitted, and wearies the doorkeeper with his importunity." He "sacrifices all he has, however valuable, to bribe the doorkeeper." This situation continues throughout the man's life. "As he grows old, he only grumbles to himself. He becomes childish, and, since in his long years' contemplation of the doorkeeper he has come to know even the flees in his fur collar, he begs the fleas to help him change the doorkeeper's mind." Curiously, the man from the country never tries to actually enter the gate. He only asks for permission to do so. Despite his continual efforts to transgress the limits dictated by the language of the doorkeeper, the man from the country nevertheless presupposes that these limits have an absolute value and that, as long as these limits exist, his desire to enter the gate cannot, in principle, be realized.

The man from the country embraces the limits posed by the language of the doorkeeper without pondering the question of what freedom—his freedom—may mean in the face of these limits. As the man from the country sees it, without the doorkeeper's permission there is simply no place for his own freedom. The doorkeeper's words are a pure and total prohibition. And in internalizing this prohibition so unquestioningly, the man from the country does not recognize that, in addition to exercising a veto, the doorkeeper has ultimately done nothing to stop him from entering. Indeed, the gate to the Law "stands open as usual" all along. The man fails to see that just as the gate has never been shut before him so the question of his freedom remains open for him to explore. The man from the country focuses on the impossibility of entrance to the Law as asserted in the language of the doorkeeper and never actually attempts to investigate or challenge it. He never dares explore the consequences of leaving the sphere of possibility embodied in the doorkeeper's language ("it is not possible . . . it may be possible later," etc.) and placing, instead, a foot in actuality, that is, trying to step through the gate. For the man from the country the question of freedom is ultimately a question of facts. He accepts the negation of his freedom as one accepts the givenness of a fact: this is how things are. And, in this respect, the man from the country offers an example of how we can trivialize the question of freedom. Moreover, by treating the limitations of his situation in a manner that allegedly frees him from the burden of freedom, the man from the country absolves himself of any real responsibility to realize that freedom and his self-determination as an individual. He disputes the restrictive structure of reality, its prohibitions, and the impossibility presented in the statements of the doorkeeper. At the same time, he clings to these disputed restrictions in order to avoid (the possibility of becoming) himself. The man from the country hides from responsibility, from becoming an individual, from leading a creative life. His hiding place is the virtuality of propositional language. "So how does it happen," asks the man before dying "that for all these many years no one but myself has ever begged admittance?" And the doorkeeper answers with the bottom line of this parable, a bottom line that surprises us—but does it really surprise the man from the country? "No one else could ever be admitted here, since this gate was made only for you."¹³

6. From Disappointment to Philosophy

Can we locate a perspective that would illuminate freedom in language? How would it be possible to embrace Kierkegaard's critique of the propositional without internalizing the opposition between an individual's freedom in language and the hegemony of the propositional? We may begin to answer these questions by taking another look at the Kierkegaardian aphorism that has established the parameters for our investigation.

> What philosophers say about reality is often as disappointing as a sign you see in a shop window, which reads: Pressing Done Here. If you brought your clothes to be pressed, you would be fooled; for the sign is for sale.¹⁴

Our interpretation of this parable has tied Kierkegaard's apparent disappointment with philosophy to his critique of the language of philosophy. We have emphasized the failure of philosophical language to engage the problem of existence, a failure that stems from the intrinsic limitations of language and particularly from the propositional infrastructure of language that remains general, public, abstract, and hypothetical. Philosophy's language, we argued, resembles the sign in the window not only in its inability to represent the reality that concerns the individual but also in the disappointment it causes to the trusting individual. In this context we have suggested that, for Kierkegaard, silence, paradox, and indirect communication are forms of opposition against the limitations that language places on philosophy. Is there another direction we can take, a direction that does not stand in opposition to our everyday experience of language?

We may tentatively identify such a possibility by relocating the focus of Kierkegaard's aphorism. There is an important aspect of Kierkegaard's parable that we have not yet addressed. It is the question concerning the source of the individual's disappointment. This is equivalent to asking about the individual's responsibility for his disappointment. We have noted how the individual is disappointed when he is misled by a sign in the window. And, yet, has he really been misled? Can we truly understand disappointment without examining the complexity of expectations from which disappointment issues?

While the individual was obviously misled by the sign, he was not in any way deceived. There was nothing deceptive about the sign or its place in the window. The background for, both, his misunderstanding and his disappointment was the expectation that the sign would function differently. He expected the sign to be a representation, but it was not. More to the point, he was misguided by the language of the sign because he failed to take its specific workings into account. His initial response to the sign was governed by an oversimplified conception of language, one too narrow to accommodate the richness of language's field of usability and one that fails to respond to the contingent singularity of the phenomenon.

Can we now read the Kierkegaardian aphorism so that it illuminates—perhaps in spite of Kierkegaard—not only the disappointment evoked by the language of philosophy but the connection between such disappointment and a fixed preconception of what language is and should be? Can we understand Kierkegaard's position regarding philosophical language not only in terms of the disappointing structure of the propositional but also as an expression of the tendency to take this hegemonic structure for granted? I think it would be wrong to try and commit Kierkegaard to a definitive position on this issue. We may nevertheless notice that the disappointment with language he describes is experienced by an individual who is predisposed to accept a reductive picture of language that is dominated by a single unifying structure: the form of propositions. What makes the position of this Kierkegaardian individual to language problematic is not only its basis in a partial picture of language. More important, this problematic is born of the individual's tendency to relate to the structure of language as if it were a given fact, one that leaves no question in regard to the individual's place in language. Very much like Kafka's man from the country, Kierkegaard's individual experiences the disappointment of language as a result of having allowed language to determine the horizons of his freedom. He has adopted the structure of language as the structure of his own expectations and has consequently absolved himself of responsibility for his own life with language. Disappointment is a mood imprisoned by the past and resentful of the future.

In being disappointed, the Kierkegaardian individual shows that the grounds for his rapport with language have taken the form of predetermined standards all along, standards that bar the individual from experiencing language's openness—or his own openness through language—to the possibility of the new. The proper way to put this is to say that what is crucially missing in the way the disappointed individual relates to language is an awareness of creativity. And this is precisely the possibility we are searching for. That is, in the search for the personal, we cannot afford to be disappointed by the structural limits of our (philosophical) language. On the contrary, we should recognize our encounter with language's limits as the very place where philosophy can become, and should become, creative. The limits of language may be experienced as restrictive and confining and can awaken, along with other responses such as frustration, irony, dreams of transcendence, that "impulse" of which Wittgenstein speaks: "to run up against." But the limits of language may also be experienced as a form of freedom. This is where philosophical creativity begins.

CHAPTER 3
Austin's Fireworks

To feel the firm ground of prejudice slipping away is exhilarating, but brings its revenges. —J. L. Austin, How to Do Things with Words

The personal needs to be thought together with the question—with the open possibility—of freedom in language. Can I, how can I, what would it mean, in language, with limits, for me to be free? As suggested, these questions open up quite naturally to the issue of responsibility: What do I do in the face of freedom? How do I orient myself in relation to the promise of a possible freedom in language as well as in relation to the actual horizons opened by freedom? Again, what would it mean, for me, to exercise the kind of freedom I have in language? As long as these questions remain unopen the propositional shall continue to rule. To put this in another way, we may say that although the subversion of the rule of propositions is an essential condition for hearing the personal, such subversion alone does not, in itself, open up the personal. In fact, the act of undoing the propositional may easily—indeed, may very likely—result in recreating its indifference toward the personal. That is, from our perspective, stepping off the firm ground of prejudice, the prejudice of the propositional, might, in Austin's words, "bring its revenges."

And, in fact, the several outstanding attempts by twentieth-century philosophy to overcome the hegemony of propositions have all ultimately failed to consequently respond to the personal.

There is a negative lesson to be gleaned from the ways these critical alternatives have failed to make a place for the personal. This chapter focuses on the pragmatic turn inaugurated in the work of J.L. Austin, which provides a clear view on one of the twentieth-century's dramatic shifts in the conceptualization of language. This is a shift (manifest in a variety of both Continental and Anglo-American approaches) away from from the spectatorial and intellectualist presuppositions of Cartesian epistemology and, in particular, away from a model of language based on the notion of cognitive representation to an understanding of language as a medium for actions or deeds, a medium, or an instrument, that articulates itself through force and effect and whose underpinning is fundamentally pragmatic.

1. Austin's Fireworks: The Promise of the Pragmatic Turn

In the concluding lecture of *How to Do Things with Words*, J. L. Austin looks back at the course of his investigation. At "this point" where he "could do no more than explode a few hopeful fireworks," he proposes the following morals:

> (A) The total speech act in the total speech situation is the *only actual* phenomenon which, in the last resort, we are engaged in elucidating.
> (B) Stating, describing, &c., are just two names among a very great many others for illocutionary acts; they have no unique position.[1]

These conclusions are not just a reminder for Austin of the scope of the project he undertook in *How to Do Things with Words*. They are meant to open up, or, as the metaphoric "fireworks" suggest, to illuminate a horizon of investigation that philosophy needs to recognize in setting the field for its inquiry into language. Austin is presenting, in other words, a new agenda for the philosophy of language. He is sketching the topography of a new question zone, doing so with an awareness that finds expression not only in the programmatic style of *How to Do Things with Words* but also in such explicit formulations as we find in the text's closing passage. Here Austin speaks with typical irony about what he has been doing and did "not altogether like doing," that is, "producing a programme, that is, saying what ought to be done rather than doing something."[2]

Austin is a philosopher who uniquely undertook the role of rebelling against the reign of the propositional. At the same time, he understands that the hegemony of the propositional is not just another philosophical thesis to be criticized or refuted. The propositional does not derive its authority from any specific philosophical argument. It cannot, therefore, be overturned by counterargument. In other words, since the propositional dominates the very construction of speech as a philosophical subject matter, breaking out of its hold requires a shift in the constitutive perspective by which philosophy paradigmatically frames the problem of language. For Austin, then, the possibility of overturning the propositional depends on how philosophy defines its investigation of language: how it frames the subject matter to begin with. And so, when turning to reflect on speech, philosophy must note Austin's first moral, namely, that its object of investigation is an "actual phenomenon." In light of Austin's passion for conciseness, the juxtaposition of such significance-laden terms as *actual* and *phenomenon*—terms that are not only verbose, but are part of a traditional metaphysical vocabulary—cannot itself be without meaning. These terms must be serving to make a specific point. That point, as I understand it, is that language should not be investigated as if it were an abstract possibility or an object already belonging to the sphere of the thinkable. If we are to read into Austin a phenomenological sensitivity (which he is clearly deserving of),[3] we can say that he is motivated by the need to make a place for the way in which language makes itself heard.

Once language is allowed to appear as a phenomenon, it manifests itself, according to Austin, in the form of speech or, more precisely, as the "total speech act in the total speech situation." Language is embodied in both "act" and "situation." The act is *in* the situation. Both act and situation appear to us, and want to be seen, in their totality. (In fact, such terms as *total* and *totality* suggest the existence of a certain tension between Austin's phenomenological concerns and his more strictly pragmatic inclinations. This tension also expresses itself in the relationship between *act*" and *situation*, a matter to which we shall return below.) For Austin, the turn toward the actual phenomenon of language, to the speech act in the speech situation, is a fundamental, even requisite, philosophical move. Its central consequence is moral (B): the possibility of releasing ourselves, of releasing language, from the sway of the propositional. According to Austin, once thematized in terms of the act and situation of speech, fact-depicting language loses its unique, and traditionally domineering, position.

When reading Austin's "morals" today, however, half a century after he delivered his lectures at Harvard, these (once) radical declarations seem to have lost their urgency. Do you sense how dated these programmatic imperatives are? Do you discern how Austin's prescriptions no longer contain the openness they presumed to have had then and that the future onto which they project themselves has turned into history, that is, the history of the philosophy of language? Indeed, if Austin's "fireworks" have lost their explosive potential—if these "hopeful fireworks" have become somewhat anachronistic (is not such a sense of anachronism integral to the beauty of fireworks?)—this is, first and foremost, because of how the philosophy of language has found a home in the pragmatic framework. Since the "pragmatic turn" in the philosophy of language, the speech act and the speech situation have emerged as central issues for philosophy. In so doing they have effected a complete remodeling of that framework in which philosophy articulates the question of meaning. What for Austin, Wittgenstein, and Ryle was a dramatic effort at breaking the grip of an ideal—of jettisoning a purely semantic—conception of language by insisting on the need to focus on the actual uses of language, on speech, on utterance and action, as well as on the ordinary, has become a truism for contemporary philosophy. It is a starting point that no longer needs to be mentioned. It is a commonplace today that any understanding of the question of meaning cannot be achieved without understanding the salient features of the speech situation, without considering the actual (the intentional and interpretative) use of language by speakers and hearers. Or, as Strawson puts it, "as theorists, we know now nothing of human *language* unless we understand human *speech*."[4]

The speech act seems to have gained the recognition Austin sought for it. His work (his insight or intuition), generally regarded as lacking a sufficient theoretical backbone, has been provided the solid post facto framework it needed, including a general theory of speech acts.[5] His *How to Do Things with Words* has been canonized as a founding text of the pragmatic-linguistic tradition. A founding text is supposed to show where it all started. And although nothing ever really starts at one specific place, what may happen at that particular place can be so dramatic (if not traumatic) that we want just the same to return there.

But upon returning to *How to Do Things with Words* we discover that, despite Austin's significant influence, the radical implications of his project were never integrated, were, in fact, disregarded by the pragmatic-linguistic tradition. That is to say, the pragmatic tradition appropriated Austin in a manner that was systematically blind to—and thus suppressing of—what I hold to be so central to his thought: the refusal to accept, if not subvert, the hegemony of the propositional. Pragmatics has made a place for a wide spectrum of speech acts. But this was done without ever questioning the inherited status of the propositionl. Moreover, it was done in a manner foreign to Austin's insight, one that wholly reasserts the "priority of the propositional," positing the propositional as the basis of its framework.

2. How to Do Things with Austin

The pragmatic tradition that followed Austin typically understood the act of language—language's structure of performativity or functionality—as a mere supplement to the propositional core of language. As a consequence, language's dimension of force is construed as a factor thematically separated from and subsequently subordinated to an independent, privileged, propositional component. The speech act is thus conventionally conceptualized, to use Searle's symbolization, as "F(p) where the variable 'F' takes illocutionary force indicating devices as values and 'p' takes expressions for propositions."[6] In other words, standard treatments of speech paradigmatically assume that utterances consist of a propositional core. What's more, it is by virtue of this propositional content that the utterance acquires any meaning at all. On the other hand, the force of utterances is understood to be a modifier that enables the (same) content, or representation, to function in a variety of ways: to make statements, ask questions, promise promises, etc. It is, thus, by means of a force-operator that a representation becomes related to the world in a particular way.[7] Force is perceived to be part of a larger pragmatic matrix that connects the propositional nucleus of an utterance to an utterance's communicative outcome.[8] And so, for example, understanding the meaningfulness of language "consists," as John McDowell puts it, "in the ability to know, when speakers produce utterances in it, what propositional acts, with what contents they are performing."[9] "Understanding a language involves knowing, on occasion, what speakers of it are doing, under descriptions which report their behavior as speech-acts of specified kinds with specified contents."[10]

Pragmatics identifies a gap between the representational foundations of an utterance's meaning (which semantics addresses) and the actual manifestation of meaning in the speech situation.[11] It thus treats the utterance's force as a factor to be included in attempting to supplement the semantic analysis and bridge this gap. The need to account for speech by considering the act's pragmatic conditions and not only its semantics is taken to be Austin's central lesson. It is understood, more generally, to be the main thrust of the pragmatic turn (which means that Austin's insight becomes a mere supplement to semantics). In this respect, the propositional hegemony characteristic of semantics has taken on a new form following the "pragmatic turn," a form not immediately apparent because of the general recognition of the diversity of the domain of speech acts as an important feature of language's functionality. This means, in fact, that the reign of propositions is even stronger in pragmatics than in traditional semantics. The hegemony of propositions is so inherent to pragmatics that the structure of all speech acts—not just statements, but the structure of promises and jokes, of insults, apologies, complaints, of flattery, courting, words of defiance, of protest, etc.—is posited as propositional in its essence. While propositions are associated in traditional semantics with basically one sentential structure, in pragmatics they play a constitutive role in constructing the whole range of the speech act. (From another perspective, this means that propositions come to govern the linguistic phenomenon from behind the scenes. They are given a constitutive role because they do not reveal themselves in the actual manifestation of speech.) In a pragmatically-oriented philosophy of language, the propositional structure has become an infrastructure.

In turning again to Austin and his reception by the philosophical tradition, we may think of the philosophical effect he has had on the tradition in the light of that metaphor of exploding fireworks which appears in the conclusion of *How to Do Things with Words*. Fireworks do not explode for no reason. Austin knew that the discovery of the performativity of language was a special day for philosophy. It was a philosophical "moment," or occasion, to which Austin hoped philosophy would rise. In introducing the speech act, Austin foresaw the possibility of a radical conceptual change in our understanding of language. But since his work did not have the form of a standard theory and was thus not tangible enough for the tradition to grasp onto, it could do no more than momentarily illuminate the field with new festive colors that then fade without ever being fully registered or captured. They leave, at best, a scant, suggestive trace. Austin's work left an impression, but its more radical suggestions were too ephemeral to be appropriated by the tradition.

We now need to look more closely at how recognition of the speech act served Austin in breaking out of the propositional paradigm. We can begin this task by considering how the speech act is born or, more specifically, how Austin's discovery of the performative makes it possible to understand that the act rather than the proposition is the underlying form of language.

3. The Act of Speech

Austin opens *How to Do Things with Words* with the stated aim of studying a particular linguistic phenomenon that, in his view, had not received enough specific consideration. "The phenomenon to be discussed is very widespread and obvious, and it cannot fail to have been already noticed, at least here and there, by others." "Yet I," he continues, "have not found attention paid to it specifically."[12] What was so unusually important for Austin is now a commonplace: a type of sentence in the first-person singular indicative that "do[es] not 'describe' or 'report' or 'constate' anything at all, [is] not 'true or false.'" These sentences are performatives (5).

Performative sentences, according to Austin, cannot be true or false precisely because they "do not 'describe' or 'report' or 'constate,'" that is, because they do not relate to the world in a way that makes them candidates for truth: they do not represent the state of things, nor are they uttered in order to depict or deny facts. They do something else. In fact, what distinguishes performative sentences is that they do—that they participate in the world by doing.

Austin's preliminary examples of the performative are the following:

(E.a) 'I do (sc. Take this woman to be my lawful wedded wife)'—as uttered in the course of the marriage ceremony.

(E.b) 'I name this ship the *Queen Elizabeth*'—as uttered when smashing the bottle against the stem.

(E.c) 'I give and bequeath my watch to my brother'—as occuring in a will.

(E.d) 'I bet you sixpence it will rain tomorrow' (5).

When considering each of these sentences, according to Austin, we see that none provide a depiction of facts or a description of the state of affairs. Sentence E.b, for example, is not a depiction of the fact that the speaker is naming a ship. Similarly, sentence E.d is not a description of the speaker placing a bet on tomorrow's weather. What these sentences do, instead, is take part in an act (naming a ship, placing a bet) that brings about a certain state of affairs.

Austin does not try to demonstrate the difference between performatives and fact-depicting sentences (or "constatives" in Austin's terms) by means of argumentation or analysis. There is no place for such argumentation because the difference between these two modalities of language should be clear to anyone who looks at them. "It needs argument no more than that 'damn' is not true or false" (6). Austin's use of examples is precisely the means to get one to look. (In this respect, his method is very much in the spirit of Wittgenstein's imperative, "Don't think, look!")

Austin made an atraditional move in calling attention to the distinctive character of the performative, for he claimed a place of philosophical importance for a mode of linguistic expression, a domain of language, that does not depict facts. This was not his sole objective. Austin did not suggest we look at any of the philosophically "peripheral" linguistic regions traditionally distinguished from propositions. He is not referring us to optatives, interogatives, imperatives, nor to any other kind of sentence grammatically distinct from propositions. Austin is not concerned with the linguistic domains relegated by semantics to the margins of the language-field. Instead, he focuses on a particular kind of nondescriptive sentence he identifies as belonging *within* the very same boundaries of the linguistic domain that semantics circumscribes as its subject matter. He has chosen to fish for performatives in the depth of the propositional sea.

Austin's discovery of the performative results from a reopening of the question about what exactly the tradition includes in the propositional domain. Such a rethinking makes it clear, he argues, that not all sentences that customarily pass as propositions are actually so. Not all sentences traditionally regarded as part of the propositional domain belong there (2). And so, the very first thing Austin tells us about the kind of sentences he wants to typify is that their apparent identity (as propositions) is misleading. Performative sentences are presented by Austin as "masqueraders," sentences that commonly "masquerade as a statement of fact, descriptive or constative" (4). In using the term *masqueraders* Austin does not imply that performatives belong to a linguistic form distinct from statements of fact. On the contrary, the performative is a type of sentence whose own grammatical form (i.e., first person, present, indicative) not only appears to be fact stating but is actually indistinguishable from that of fact-statements.[13] The performative sentence is most commonly mistaken for constative "oddly enough, when it assumes its most explicit form" (4).

The performative is a kind of sentence whose identity is haunted by the proposition. (As we shall see, however, this also means that the identity of fact-depicting language is haunted by performativity.) To individuate the performative thus means to distinguish it from its propositional double. This is what Austin aims to accomplish in the first part of his investigation. "It will be convenient therefore, to study it [the performative] first in this misleading form, in order to bring out its characteristics by contrasting them with those of the statement of fact which it apes" (4). And, indeed, after a "preliminary isolation of the performative" which is "provisional and subject to revision in the light of later sections" (4)—the observation that performatives "are not true or false," they are, or are "part of, the doing of an action" (5).

Austin turns to examine possible ways in which the distinction between performatives and statements of fact could be tangibly constructed. This search for a defining criterion of the performative develops into the central theme, and the guiding principle, of *How to Do Things with Words*. It turns out to be an unfulfilled search, however.

After examining a series of candidates that all fail to individuate the performative, Austin pauses in lecture 6 to reflect on whether there exist certain kinds of candidates that, in principle, cannot perform this role. Citing his inability to define the performative, Austin recognizes that his attempt to do so by means of "a criterion or criteria of grammar or of vocabulary or of both" is a structural impossibility.

> We pointed out that there was certainly no one absolute criterion of this kind: and that very probably it is not possible to lay down even a list of all possible criteria; moreover, they certainly would not distinguish performatives from constatives, as very commonly the *same* sentence is used on different occasions of utterance in *both* ways, per-

formative and constative. The thing seems hopeless from the start, if we are to leave utterances *as they are* and seek for a criterion (67).

Grammatical criteria, according to Austin, do not suffice in distinguishing performatives from constatives because the difference between these two types of utterances is not always manifest on a merely linguistic level. Performatives and factual statements are often indistinguishable at the level of their linguistic form. The clearest evidence for this are cases in which a grammatically identical sentence functions, "on different occasions of utterance," as both a performative and a proposition. And yet, the fact that the same sentence functions "in both ways" does not only indicate the intrinsic inapplicability of grammatical criteria to the task of capturing the difference between performatives and propositions. It also shows that this difference cannot be perceived as long as we deal with the sentences of a language in abstraction from the context of their actual use (the speech situation). The sentence in itself—the context-independent linguistic unit—is too thin a medium to provide sufficient grounds for making the distinction at stake. From another perspective this means that if the distinction between performative and propositional form can be at all constructed, it depends on a view that would allow language to present itself in a richer manner than that of the ideal linguistic sentence entity. The need thus arises to jettison the ideality of the context-free sentence and move toward an understanding of the actual linguistic utterance—"the actual phenomenon"—which creates a place for its intrinsic embeddedness in the speech situation. In lecture 7 of *How to Do Things with Words*, then, Austin announces the need to "make a fresh start on the problem," and he turns to examine "the senses in which to say something may be to do something, or in saying something we do something" (91). For Austin, the shift toward the actuality of language, toward language in its actuality, implies a new focus on language's act-quality. This recognition, or responsiveness, to language as an "actual phenomenon" is ultimately equivalent to recognizing language qua its functionality or use, being open to language as a domain of action and deeds. This is how the "speech act" is born.[14]

The thematization of speech as an act contains two aspects. The speech act opens an avenue for exploring the identity of the performative. At the same time, it marks the need to problematize the way semantics construes fact-depicting sentences. Although Austin is concerned with the individuation of the performative, the lack of a sufficiently strong basis for distinguishing between constatives and performatives means that—on an ideal basis—the individuation of statements is just as problematic, that the homogeneity of the propositional cannot be upheld. In particular, it does not allow for the historically established identity between fact-stating and the domain created by the grammatical category of declarative sentences.[15] Austin's move may be read, in other words, as an implicit critique of an ideal conception of language (semantics) that fails to sustain the cohesiveness of its domain (propositions). The semantic framework, strict as it aspires to be, is vulnerable to external elements that undermine the ostensible homogeneity of its domain. In this respect, recognizing the speech act not only departs from a semantic-linguistic picture too narrow to accommodate the performative. It also fulfills a need that is crucial for grounding the identity of propositional language, which is just as dependent on its embeddedness in the *act*ual utterance.

For Austin, in contrast to the tradition that followed him, the primacy of the speech act implies that in making a place for fact-depicting language the propositional will be deprived of its traditional privileged status. This will consequently undermine its hegemony. Once the primacy of the speech act—of speech qua act—is embraced, fact-depicting language must also be understood in terms of its embeddedness in the domain of linguistic action. However, fact-stating acts do not have a particularly central place in this new domain because they are, before anything else, acts. Fact-depicting utterances can no longer dominate language's spectrum of functionality because stating a fact is neither more common nor more fundamental an act than, for instance, promising, warning, urging, opposing, or announcing. As we have seen Austin explain in his concluding morals, "Stating, describing, &c., are *just two* names among a very great many others for illocutionary acts; they have no unique position" (149).

As suggested above, Austin diverges here from the tradition that appropriated his work, a tradition that, while embracing language's spectrum of usability, was unable to understand—or not interested in understanding—how or why that would challenge the privileged status of the propositional. (That is, a tradition that insisted on interpreting the pragmatic underpinning of language from a point of view that remains committed to the propositional.) Indeed, as the morals of *How to Do Things with Words* suggest, Austin did not consider the possibility of integrating language's spectrum of usability into a philosophical framework that would constitute the crux of his work. He was concerned, rather, with the manner in which a new focus on "the *actual phenomenon* of language" enables philosophy to listen to and hear language in ways philosophy had not done so before. For him, the most important aspect of the pragmatic insight is how it opens a completely new perspective for language to show itself to us. What is revealed is that, like performatives, constatives too never cease participating in the human situation. They are never at rest from doing something. Or, in Austin's words, "once we realize that what we have to study is not the sentence but the issuing of an utterance in a speech situation, there can hardly be any longer a possibility of not seeing that stating is performing an act" (139).

The language of facts can describe, report, tell, narrate, evaluate, judge, predict, or quote, among other activities. Regardless of its specific use, this language is trapped in a form of functionality that precedes the ideality of content and serves as the basis for the meaningfulness of its utterances. In other words, the new focus on the speech act not only allows Austin to resist, or hold in abeyance, the paradigmatic tendency to anchor language in the ideality of content or representation. It also gives expression to an alternative view of language, one that develops from the recognition of speech as never neutral in terms of its involvement or participation in the human situation. Language, according to this view, is fundamentally involved, and already so before being anything else: it bears the form of participation before it says anything in particular.

In this respect, what makes Austin's pragmatic turn so radical is not (just) the addition of a practical axis to our conceptualization of the phenomenon of language. Rather, it is Austin's responsiveness to the primacy of the situatedness of language, to the entanglement of language in the human situation. Language, according to Austin, is involved in everyday life in ways not only irreducible to but also more basic than the propositional form. Putting this in Heideggerian terms, to which I shall turn in more depth in the next chapter, we may say that the abstract intelligibility of cognitive, semantically structured content is of derivative form and that assertion—or statements—are "a derivative mode of interpretation."[16]

In Austin's terms, however, this means that the possibility of saying something is always grounded in, and is therefore necessarily dependent on, the gravity of those daily forms of human activity and interaction through which language participates and is manifest in ordinary life. More specifically, this means that the "locutionary act"—"which is roughly equivalent to uttering a certain sentence with a certain sense and reference, which again is roughly equivalent to 'meaning' in the traditional sense" (109)—is ultimately rooted in the field of "illocutionary acts." That is to say, that

> to perform a locutionary act is . . . *eo ipso* to perform an *illocutionary act*, as I propose to call it. Thus in performing a locutionary act we shall also be performing such an act as: asking or answering a question, giving some information or an assurance or a warning, announcing a verdict or an intention, pronouncing a sentence, making an appointment or an appeal or a criticism, making an identification of giving a description, and the numerous like. *(98–99)*

Furthermore, it is important for Austin to make clear that the relation between the locutionary and illocutionary aspects of speech cannot simply be understood in terms of the relation between what we say and how we say it. The kind of entailment connecting the locutionary to the illocutionary act—the *"eo ipso"* or the particular sense of "in" in the formula *"In* saying x I was doing y"—is indicative, according to Austin, of a constitutive relation that does not permit us to think of the locutionary as a conceptually independent aspect of the speech act. The illocutionary, in other words, is not the external form of a given contentful utterance. It is, rather, the gravitational center of the utterance, the source of language's vivacity. It is, in other words, the underlying current through—and only through—which "meaning in the favorite philosophical sense of that word" (94) can display itself as such. Once we recognize the illocutionary force as the true élan—the internal movement—of speech, we shall also see that the notion of propositional content, rooted in the possibility of a strictly cognitive depiction of facts, is externally imposed on our everyday experience. We shall see that it is a synthetic (fabricated) construction that remains insensitive to our life with language and, consequently, cannot serve as a starting point for understanding the phenomenon. More specifically, we realize that the propositional structure of content is, in itself, too general and too abstract to be the source of the meaningfulness of actual utterances. In other words, a strictly fact-depicting linguistic component cannot be individuated because the "truth and falsity of a statement depends not merely on the meanings of words but on what act you were performing in what circumstances" (145). The illocutionary, then, necessarily pervades the locutionary, doing so in a manner that does not permit us to determine the meaning of an utterance's words independently of the particular illocutionary act that is performed on the occasion of that utterance. And so the prioritization of the propositional, according to Austin, issues from "an over-simplified notion of correspondence with the facts. . . . This is the ideal of what would be right to say in all circumstances, for any purpose, to any audience, &c." (146). Austin sees the philosophical privileging of facts, or of cognitive content, to be symptomatic of a kind of reflection that fails to respond to the actuality of language (the *actual phenomenon*). This reflection empties ordinary experience of its intricacy because its attitude to "real life" is regulated by "the simple situations envisaged in logical theory" (143).

4. The Pragmatic and the Personal

One particularly relevant way of fleshing out the significance of Austin's notion of the illocutionary is to observe that, before language even stands in relation to the world of facts—before it conveys any determinate content—it already functions meaningfully by virtue of the place it occupies—the role it plays—between speaker and audience. In other words, the I-you (more generally, the human intersubjective relation) and not language's relation vis-à-vis a world of neutral facts (e.g., a relation of representation based on the sense and reference of words) is the fundamental axis along which language's meaningfulness revolves. But despite Austin's insistence on recognizing this intersubjective interaction as the origin of meaningfulness, and despite his unique resistance to the propositional, the personal is never given a place in the alternative pragmatic picture of language he proposes.

The question of the personal—of the speaker's singular presence in the things he or she says—never becomes an issue for Austin. This is no coincidence. It would not be wrong to say that Austin was simply uninterested in the question that concerns us here. But there is a structural aspect to Austin's pragmatic understanding of language—in my view, a structural aspect of pragmatics as such—that excludes the possibility of pondering the personal.

This is because Austin's pragmatic framework remains fully committed to a conception of intelligibility that is essentially public, average, and general, despite its radical shift away from the model of fact depiction. While Austin's paradigm allows us to rethink the phenomenon of language as one no longer governed by the propositional telos of transmitting semantically structured contents, the publicness and averageness of intelligibility (regulated by the averageness of the practical goals of language) remain the unquestionable, essential cornerstone of his analysis of speech acts. More specifically, we need to remember that "illocutionary acts are conventional acts" (121) for Austin. The embodiment of language in the act should be understood, to quote Habermas's favorable reading of Austin, "on the basis of institutionally bound speech acts such as baptizing, betting, appointing, and the like, in which the obligations issued from the speech act are unambiguously regulated by accompanying institutions or norms of action."[17] For Habermas, who seeks to uncover an ethical component in communicative action, Austin's notion of linguistic interaction is especially fruitful. It retains the purposefulness of the linguistic encounter while jettisoning object manipulation as its model. Speakers do not relate to their hearers as if they were objects. "Speaker and hearer, by contrast, adopt a performative attitude in which they encounter one another as members of the intersubjectively shared lifeworld of their linguistic community."[18] From our perspective, however, this is precisely what makes Austin ultimately disappointing. Just as for most of the Anglo-American philosophy of language (and, in this case, for Habermas as well), for Austin too the meaningfulness of the encounter between speaker and hearer is derived from an interaction between structurally identical linguistic agents: between members of a linguistic community for whom "sharing a lifeworld" means having an equivalent standing within a uniform, homogeneous (i.e., average) domain of intelligibility. Woven into the heart of human interaction, the meaningfulness of language is manifest in the nuanced matrix of intersubjective relations that Austin classifies in great detail. Having a language, one may—adopting Austin's examples of "exercitives"—appoint, degrade, or demote; warn, advise, or plead; pray, entreat, or beg; urge, press, or recommend; enact, reprieve, or veto (155–156). One can do, of course, much more—Austin's lists are long and open-ended. When you give me advice, for instance, or make a promise in the Austinian speech situation, the meaningfulness of your language—of the speech act you perform—is constituted of general norms: conventional or institutional codes of behavior. As such, the act is divorced from who you or I specifically are. Your speech may either realize its communicative telos or fail to do so. Regardless, the force of your speech and the effect it has on me (as the person hearing you) belong entirely to, and so do not at all transcend, the common domain of average publicness. She *promised*. You *warned* me. I *doubted*. He *begged*, and I finally *agreed*. But this kind of interaction contains no place for, no trace of, and no relevance to my singular, even idiosyncratic, being in language. It has no connection with the manner in which you, being who *you* are, inhabit *your* speech or to the way her language is affected by who *she* is. In Austin's world, what gives her promise meaning is that she promises as one promises.

When he begs, the meaningfulness of his linguistic action is constituted by the fact that he begs as one begs. There's nothing more to it. And if I doubt it, my doubts will essentially mean the same thing as the doubts of anyone else in my position. According to this picture, my language is never mine. It never issues from the singularity of my existence. Language is, indeed, always there for me to use. But it remains completely indifferent to the particularity, or peculiarity, of my attachment to my words. It bears no mark of the fact that I, and not just anyone who happens to be in a similar situation, am the singular speaker. In this respect, those laws concerning the circulating currency of money—that it is impartial and unerringly the same for whoever uses it—are true of Austin's language as well. ("My money is just as good as anyone else's," shouts the ragged bum being ignored by the elegant staff at a fancy store.) This means that the speech act is essentially neutral. Just as money "has no smell," Austin's language act is also free of partiality or prejudice. It might be performed by a particular speaker, but it remains completely unaffected by the individual's speech.

We can put this another way: Austin's pragmatic shift redefines language's teleology. It reorganizes language under a new telos. Austin's understanding of language as a field of intersubjective, conventional interaction posits the relation between act and effect, between means and ends, as the basis for understanding the meaningfulness—the meaningful workings—of language. In so doing, however, Austin necessarily reproduces a model that encourages philosophers of language to interpret the telos of communication as the transmission of cognitive content. For Austin, no less than for the tradition he criticizes, the philosophical reconstruction of the so-called speech situation is a limited, even dull, picture of human experience, one that flattens the world of language by presenting it as fundamentally equivalent to a functional, conventionally governed setting. In this setting competent "language users," or "language practitioners," perform acts to achieve specific—practical or theoretical—ends. The significance of these acts can be learned from a given public lexicon. Their purpose is no less determined by average common sense. Austin may resist a representational, or content-based, view of speech. Nevertheless, his functional understanding of human linguistic interaction invariably leads to a narrow, instrumental telos governed by public standards of success. This locates speech as occurring between agents whose relation to their language, not to mention their relation to themselves, and to each other, is necessarily external.[19]

Furthermore, in spite of Austin's critical response to the hegemony of the propositional, his thinking about language remains captive to the propositional form. True, Austin's work allows philosophy to articulate the modus operandi of language in terms not derived from traditional relations of fact depiction. As we've seen, Austin's insistence on the primacy of the speech act goes hand in hand, together with his critique of fact depiction, with what he presents as the internal mechanism by which language encounters meaning. "Once we realize that what we have to study is not the sentence but the issuing of an utterance in a speech situation, there can hardly be any longer a possibility," according to Austin, "of not seeing" that the meaningfulness of language stems from language's essential rootedness in ordinary forms of human interaction (139). The act, unlike the sentence, is an embodied linguistic unit that cannot be understood independently of the behavioral and practical matrix to which it integrally belongs. Thus, "the act is constituted not . . . by fact, essentially, but by *convention* (which is, of course, a fact)" (128). But this is precisely where the propositional finds its way back into Austin's picture. Although he releases the internal mechanisms of language from the strict bounds constituted by a (representational) relation to facts, Austin's speech act itself takes on the form of a fact. The meaningfulness of the act as an act thus appears between us in that monolithic, fully constituted form that we recognize as belonging to the order of the propositional and that, as such, can be accounted for in terms of strictly factual language. In what you've just said to me, for example, you have performed an act whose meaning is graspable as the content of the statement "In saying x you were doing y": you were either promising (or not), warning (or not), threatening (or not), insinuating (or not), etc. Or, as Austin contends, since "there is a convention here . . . —a judge could decide" (128, n. 1).

5. The Mirror at Hand: Afterthoughts

Austin's discovery of the performative, and his insistence on the primacy of performativity has paved the way to a new, and immensely influential, understanding of language. In thinking about Austin's innovation, I am invariably reminded of an analogous gesture depicted in an old comic book that came into my possession and that captured my childhood imagination. The comic book contained two stories of the Wild West that both climaxed in a shoot out. The first, which I would probably find the more riveting today, described the dilemmas of a sheriff who must face the consequences of his past life as an outlaw. But it was the second story that most captivated me then. The secret to its appeal was the fact that its protagonist was not a gunman at all, and certainly not the fastest draw in town. The hero did, however, have a natural sense of precision. This was a function of him being a responsible man. In retrospect, I am quite certain that one of the tacit morals of the story was that precision is the ultimate expression of true responsibility. In that spirit, the story's protagonist must have been an educator of sorts, even a doctor. In any event, the dramatic climax of the story occurs when our precise hero finds himself having to fight a bad guy for his life while the whole community is aware that the latter is a much quicker draw. The hero is torn over taking part in the fight. He is not the type to resolve conflicts through the barrel of a gun. But he seems this time to have little choice. As he faces his opponent, the reader is also aware that he cannot possibly defeat him. The countdown begins. But just as time runs out, the reader—the reading child—is surprised to find the hero reaching not for his gun but for a small mirror he skillfully aims in the direction of his rival's face. By means of the mirror's reflection of the sun's rays he blinds the bad guy long enough to take control of the situation. Only then does he draw his own gun and shoot, a single shot intended to disarm his opponent.

The story's innovation, of course, is the unconventional use of the mirror at hand (which depends on an understanding of the mirror-object as, to use Heidegger, *ready-to-hand*). Like Austin, the protagonist finds that a conventional medium of representation can be turned into a genuine means of action. That is, he releases the mirror (language) from its paradigmatic (passive) role as depicter of the state of things, and from its total submission to those things—to the face, the body, or the furniture in a room—that participate in the living situation. Our protagonist moves the mirror from its location at the edge of what is happening and makes a central place for it—involves it—in the event itself. As the mirror is brought into the world between us, it no longer represents the situation at hand but, rather, determines what that situation is.

Much like the comic book protagonist, Austin opens an unexpected perspective onto the ordinary (in this case, language), putting it in an entirely new light. Without ever leaving the bounds of the ordinary, Austin succeeds in uncovering a dimension of language otherwise hidden from philosophy. Austin's move does not lead him, via analysis, inference, or transcendental argument, beyond the banality of everyday phenomena. Rather, it is directed toward finding what remains unrevealed by philosophy's traditional hegemonic point of view on language. As such, it finds what "cannot fail to have been already noticed" (1). In this respect, the form of Austin's discovery matches the spirit of that which Wittgenstein says about the role of philosophy in "contributing observations that no one has doubted, but which have escaped remark only because they are always before our eyes."[20]

Moreover, Austin's "observation" is not simply an informative one. In revealing language to be a form of action, Austin not only discovers a previously unnoticed feature of language but also calls for a radical change in how philosophy frames its interest in language. By recognizing that action is a fundamental dimension of language, Austin opens up the possibility, as Wittgenstein did in his own way,[21] of refurnishing the space in which philosophy thinks about and articulates the question of meaning. However, in reacting against the reification of language by the rule of the propositional, Austin ironically arrives at a very similar position. For although the Austinian speech act allows us to experience the situatedness of language, it does this only at the expense of experiencing language as a reified instrument—and of ourselves as anonymous agents, users of tools. In this respect, we may say that Austin's picture of language is a mirror image of that of the propositional.

CHAPTER 4
Personal Objects

Truth is never gathered from objects that are present and ordinary. —Martin Heidegger, "Origin of the Work of Art"

1. Heidegger (Before) and (After) Austin

The pragmatic turn in the philosophy of language opened up the possibility for breaking out of the hegemony of the propositional. This did not happen, however. The Anglo-American tradition that appropriated the work of Austin and Wittgenstein was not interested in the more radical implications of their work and has ultimately interpreted the pragmatic turn as a philosophical adjustment: an enriching supplement to semantics. But even if the philosophy of language were to follow Austin, for example, and embrace the pragmatic turn in order to subvert the reign of the propositional, it would most likely have remained deaf to the claims of the personal. That is to say, the shift to the pragmatic, in spite of its radical potential in subverting the propositional, and in spite of the nonpropositional vision of language it seems to imply, remains distant from and external to the actual reverberation of the personal within language.

The pragmatic vision of language is blind to the personal because, as we learned in reading Austin, it is structurally indifferent to the problem of individuality. It seeks, rather, to construe the phenomenon of meaning as an exclusively public, or general, manifestation. In Heideggerian terms, we may say that the alternative offered by the pragmatic turn remains bound by the public averageness of the "they," much like the propositional picture that it contests. The philosophical attempt to ground meaning in the pragmatic, in fact, promotes a kind of absorption in the ordinary that entirely obliterates the question of the ontological difference or the problem of being an individual.

We have now arrived at Heidegger's door. This is no coincidence. It is probably clear by now that Heidegger is uniquely significant, in more ways than one, to the path I am seeking (or following?) in this book. But, in order to understand what makes Heidegger's thinking particularly relevant at this point of the argument, we need to understand how he complicates such a pragmatic picture as Austin's, and how this relates to the original motivations for our discussion of the pragmatic in the first place. We need, in particular, to see how Heidegger's position on the pragmatic is structurally similar to Kierkegaard's understanding of the propositional: how, while accepting the accuracy of a pragmatic picture such as Austin's, he also rejects it as an uncritical reproduction of our imprisonment in the average forms of everyday language.

Let us, thus, recapitulate the move we've made so far. The propositional holds us captive. It dominates language in a manner that bars us from encountering the personal. But recognizing our captivity in language is often wedded to, as our reading of Kierkegaard has shown, a problematic picture of captivity based on a strict opposition between language's (propositionally structured) "inside" and its (nonpropositional) "outside." This is an opposition between a public field of ordinary intelligibility in which there is ultimately no place for the truth of the individual and the outskirts of the intelligible in which the presentation and ineffability of that truth are paradoxically intertwined. With Kierkegaard we've seen that the propositional determines a standard for language that does not allow for the possibility of genuine individuality to materialize in the spoken. At the same time, we've also learned that a struggle or protestation against the propositional may prove to be no less problematic when motivated, and regulated, by a conception of language that allows the hegemony of the propositional to appear as the absolute negation of the individual's freedom in language.

The lesson we've learned from Kierkegaard is therefore twofold. In searching for the personal, we not only need to untangle language from the grip of the propositional. We also need to resist the temptation of allowing the common image of a prison to dominate our thinking about our being in language. This is why the option of a pragmatic sublimation of the propositional may appear to be promising. Austin's turn toward the pragmatic actuality of language allows him, as we've seen, to suspend the hegemonic status of propositions while remaining within—never leaving nor skirting the edges of—the confines of the ordinary. Yet, while releasing language from the reign of its propositional structure, this alternative view on language has turned out to be too narrow to include the personal or make a place for the presence of individuality. However, as in the case of the propositional, here too there is the danger that our protest of the restricted nature of the pragmatic will end up internalizing the pragmatic as the ultimate standard of everyday intelligibility. This is, I think, what happens to Heidegger, for whom, in *Being and Time*, the pragmatic structure of everyday language is not only an essential feature of our human situatedness but also manifests our inevitable captivity in the ordinary. More specifically, while Heidegger—like Austin and unlike Kierkegaard—untangles language from the grip of the propositional by recovering its roots in pragmatic daily experience, he also—unlike Austin and like Kierkegaard—criticizes the structure he takes to be constitutive of everyday intelligibility by opposing it to the truth of the individual. We can put this another way and say that, despite his preoccupation with the deposition of the propositional, the reign of the pragmatic is ultimately, for Heidegger, that which constitutes our imprisonment in language.

And so Heidegger concerns us here because his turn to the pragmatic creates a philosophical junction that makes place not only for the subversion of the propositional and the uncovering of more primary forms of ordinary intelligibility but also for interpreting these ordinary forms in light of the truth of the speaking individual. At the same time, this place allows us to remain completely indifferent to the claims of the personal. There is, then, a negative lesson to be learned here in the trajectory of Heidgger's thinking, a trajectory that brings Heidegger so close and yet leaves him all too distant from the personal.

This chapter will consequently consider why Heidegger's understanding of everyday language, or, more generally, of ordinary intelligibility, leaves no room for the appearance of the personal. It will then show how the exclusion of the personal from the domain of the ordinary continues to haunt Heidegger's eventual turn to the poetic. I believe that by exposing how the expulsion of the personal reproduces itself in Heidegger's later thinking, we will be in a position to elaborate—taking the *via negativa*—that form of sensitivity (or is it a sensibility?) without which philosophy can never meet the personal.

2. Heidegger's Pragmatic Interpretation of the Ordinary

To begin thinking about the trajectory that eventually leads Heidegger to authorize the poetic rather than the ordinary as the original opening of the meaningful, we need to first say a few words about his interpretation of everyday language in *Being and Time*. Heidegger is primarily concerned with language in *Being and Time* as a phenomenon that "has its roots in the existential constitution of Dasein's disclosedness"[1] and that enables him to "bring Dasein's everydayness into view in a manner which is ontologically more primordial" (210). This means that language cannot ultimately be understood in terms of its facticity. Language is not only a manifestation of Dasein's form of life. It is never only what it is, but is also always indicative of the manner in which Dasein's form of life conceals its underlying ontological structure.

Still, if we first focus on the ontic level in which Heidegger seeks to gain access to those "ontologically more primordial" dimensions of Dasein's being-in-the-world, we see that for Heidegger the necessary horizons for studying the phenomenon are the horizons of Dasein's world. That is, for Heidegger, the situatedness of Dasein, with its worldly parameters of daily existence, is a requisite starting point for thinking about language. And so, although the phenomenon of language per se receives only limited attention in *Being and Time*—"In *Being and Time*, your discussion of language remains quite sparse, says the Japanese interlocutor to Heidegger in "Dialogue on Language"[2]—its essential features are already in place in the very manner in which Heidegger sets the stage for his discussion.

The backdrop for Heidegger's reflection on language is thus the revelation of the pragmatic form of everyday intelligibility. This revelation is made possible through a dramatic attempt to encounter philosophically a fundamental dimension of everydayness that cannot be revealed in theoretical reflection governed by "objective" categories. For Heidegger, the basic unit of "objective reflection"— the theoretical, person-independent, "object" as integrated in the form of propositions—distorts the primary meaningfulness of things. This particular form of meaning cannot be encountered philosophically as long as our perception of ordinary things remains bound by the objective prism of fully constituted objects. The ordinary demands to be viewed from a perspective that allows us to see how the meaning of everyday things originates not from their objective essence but from the place and role they occupy in the domain of human concern. In other words, for Heidegger, the appearance of ordinary meaningfulness can be engaged philosophically only through a reflective turn away from predominant patterns of disengaged theorizing, away from the framing of meaning as "present-at-hand" and toward an alternative understanding of the originality of the ordinary as "ready-to-hand."

Language is essentially situated. Its being-in-the-world is more fundamental than its specific forms of being about or of representing the world. The basic features of this situatedness are, for Heidegger as for Austin, the functional and the intersubjective forms constitutive of language. Thus, language participates and is involved in the world before it says anything in particular. As such, it primarily opens onto meaning not through the framing of representations of facts that are, in themselves, outside the order of everyday intelligibility, but, rather, as a medium that allows the intelligibility of ordinary things to articulate itself. Such a sentence as "This hammer is heavy," for example, is meaningful and effective, but its signification does not originate from the presence—the representation or the comprehension—of any kind of objective content. "This hammer is heavy" does not, according to Heidegger, depict, at least not in its original form, any factual constellation whose givenness is independent of the intelligibility of the complex patterns of our involvement with such tools as hammers. On the contrary, by saying that this hammer is heavy we are bringing to light a certain aspect of the hammer, one that can be articulated only against the background of our familiarity with such things as hammers, and only because we already know, through our practical dealings with the world, what it means for a hammer to be heavy, i.e., what it means for us to be using a heavy hammer. In other words, language is a phenomenon whose intelligibility cannot be grounded in—does not originate from—our bare cognitive or representational capacities, but ensues from the more fundamental matrix of our practical relationship with daily things.

At the same time, language is also a phenomenon whose intelligibility issues from the basic forms of our relations with others. That is to say, while opening us to the intelligibility of the world of things, the appearance of language also takes a directional form: it is always already embedded in established patterns of living with others. "Talking," according to Heidegger, "is the way in which we articulate 'significantly' the intelligibility of Being-in-the-world [to which] Being-with belongs [and] which in every case maintains itself in some definite way of concernful Being-with-one-another"(204). The meaningfulness of language is, thus, dependent on interweaving the role played by things with our interactions with other persons. That is, language appears between Dasein and its world only on the basis of Dasein's relations to others. Or, to put it differently, the appearance of meaning in language has it roots in the intersection of two constitutive dimensions of Dasein's being-in-the-world: being-in and being-with.

As Heidegger sketches the phenomenological spectrum through which language shows itself in everydayness, the affinity to Austin's speech acts becomes apparent.

> Being-with-one-another is discursive as assenting or refusing, as demanding or warning, as pronouncing, consulting, or interceding, as "making assertions" and in talking in the way of "giving a talk." *(204)*

This affinity reaches even deeper once we recognize that the outcome of framing language in this way (i.e., in terms of its interactive functionality) allows Heidegger like Austin, to thematize the workings of language in a manner that resists the hegemony of the propositional. Language allows Dasein to share with others the intelligibility of the world because the being of others is a constitutive dimension of Dasein's world, because the structure of the intelligibile is, as such, essentially shared (205). But, precisely because the averageness of language stems from our shared form of life rather than from an objective factual order, the propositional must lose its traditionally dominant position within the space of the intelligible. Hence, just as for Austin "stating, describing, &c., are *just two* names among a very great many others for illocutionary acts; they have no unique position,"[3] for Heidegger "communication in which one makes assertions—giving information, for instance—is a special case of that communication which is grasped in principle existentially" (205).

In Heidegger's conception of language the opening of a prethematic, intersubjective, yet nonobjective domain of meaning—a world—goes hand in hand with an attempt to break out of the propositional regimentation of the meaningful. But as Heidegger attends to the new horizon of meaning he uncovers, as he focuses on "the attuned intelligibility of being-in-the-world . . . expressed in discourse," Heidegger hurries, despite his explicit motivations, to reconstruct ordinary language on the surprisingly narrow basis of the strictly pragmatic. He unpacks the "concernful understanding," or the "circumspect interpretation," which he thematizes as the "origin" and grounds of everyday language in a surprisingly constricted manner. This constricted manner ultimately erases the difference between, on the one hand, the fundamental structure of concern that underlies the fact that things actually matter to us (or, more generally, that opens the world for us in ways that are never neutral) and, on the other hand, the strict instrumental forms of being invested in the world, the "kind of concern which manipulates things and puts them to use" (83). While showing how the propositional form distorts the original phenomenon of meaning and why the appearance of meaning must alternatively be explained in terms of Dasein's embeddedness or immersion in the domain of everydayness, Heidegger, much like Austin, ends up positing the form of the pragmatic as (if it were) the true heart of everyday experience. Anticipating one of the more popular maxims of the Anglo-American philosophy of language, Heidegger thus elaborates his version of "meaning is use" in a manner that may be more radical than subsequent variations, but is just as indifferent to the depths of ordinary human concern and just as unresponsive to the rich, heterogeneous character of our daily involvement with things. This leaves him particularly blind, again like Austin, to the possibility that matters to us here: the unfolding of meaning on the grounds of genuine personal involvement.

Heidegger, in other words, is probably more clear than any other twentieth-century philosopher about the need to liberate the phenomenon of meaning from the traditional "as"-structure by which propositions present an object under the sign of a predicate. He considers this necessary because the modus operandi by which statements determine and explicate the appearance of "something as something" is not only derivative but also hides a more original event(fullness) of meaning. "The 'as' does not first show up in the statement." On the contrary, the "as" made explicit in a statement "is possible only because it is *there* as something to be stated" (189). Thus, according to Heidegger, a philosophical exploration of that obscure *there* from which meaning originally grows becomes necessary. He calls upon us to explore the potential of a more primordial "as"-structure—the "as" of circumspect interpretation that understands; the existential-hermeneutical "as" (201)—that opens up the "disclosedness of understanding" in the first place. And yet, as Heidegger himself turns to this task of rooting meaning in grounds previously overshadowed by the propositional, the only alternative he finds worth developing is that opened by underpinning language in man's instrumental interaction with things. For Heidegger, the key for coming to terms with the pre-predicative or prethematic forms of everyday meaningfulness—the meaning that emerges from the heart of our daily involvement with the things we care about—is ultimately found in the form of "equipment," in "equipmentality." We can put this more directly by saying that in

Being and Time, despite a variety of gestures toward a primordial depth allegedly obscured by the propositional, the conclusive standard of everyday intelligibility is set and regulated by Heidegger's recurring image—his paradigmatic example—of a man using a hammer.

3. The Prison of the Ordinary

Heidegger, thus, much like Austin, not only embraces the pragmatic as the inner form of everyday language. He also regards the discovery of the pragmatic as a crucial philosophical move, one that liberates the ordinary from the hegemony of the propositional. Yet, while sharing a pragmatic picture of language that is similar to Austin's in crucial ways, we need to remember that Heidegger sets this picture against a completely different background. While positing the pragmatic as the characteristic structure of the ontic level of Dasein's being-in-the-world, Heidegger refuses to consider the pragmatic structure of the phenomenon of meaning to be just a positive manifestation of Dasein's being. According to Heidegger, the structure of everyday intelligibility not only reflects central aspects of Dasein's situatedness. It simultaneously conceals the possibility of a more comprehensive view of Dasein's constitution, a view that would reveal the partiality and limitations of the pragmatic form of the ordinary. In other words, everyday language can be said to be symptomatic of Dasein's existential constitution because it so clearly manifests the intelligibility of Dasein's world. But, we also need to keep in mind that, according to Heidegger, this world is as much Dasein's actual home as it indeed marks Dasein's place of captivity. It is, as such, an inevitable form of self-alienation or inauthenticity. Precisely in reflecting the actual character of the ordinary everyday language thus provides access to what Heidegger understands to be Dasein's absorption in the publicness of the "they." Ordinary language is testimony to that "mode of average everydayness" that is the form of Dasein's forgetfulness of—of its fleeing in the face of—"its ownmost potentiality-for-Being" (318).

Hence, while Austin is a philosopher who fully endorses the discovery of the pragmatic—who embraces the pragmatic as part of a philosophical *joie de vivre* or as a cause for philosophical celebration (remember the metaphor of "exploding fireworks" noted in the previous chapter)—Heidegger cannot view the pragmatic character of everyday meaningfulness without ambivalence. In this respect we may also say that Heidegger's pragmatic insight is fundamentally so much more radical than Austin's that it would ultimately be wrong to see Heidegger as a pragmatic thinker at all.

For Heidegger, the pragmatic interpretation of the ordinary goes hand in hand with his understanding of everyday language as being fundamentally equivalent to idle talk. "Idle talk . . . is the kind of being which belongs to Dasein's understanding when that understanding has been uprooted" (214). It is a form of intelligibility that cuts Dasein off from any genuine relation to itself and to its surroundings. Dasein has no access to its own voice in idle talk and so ineluctably speaks in the voice of *das Man*. Yet, as suggested, this condition of uprootedness is, in principle, not a transitory one. "This uprooting is rather Dasein's most everyday most stubborn 'Reality'" (214). This is because the "they" is not imposed on Dasein's being. The "they" does not dominate the self from outside as much as it "belongs to Dasein's positive constitution" (167). The "they," in other words, is not only what separates the self from the possibility of authenticity; it is also what constitutes the possibility of selfhood in the first place. "The Self of everyday Dasein is the *they-self*" (167).

Hence, since the language of everyday Dasein is the average language of the "they," the search for authenticity implies turning to a place unregimented by public intelligibility. For Heidegger, this turn begins with the call of conscience. The call "asserts nothing, gives no information . . . has nothing to tell," and yet, precisely because it is not "anything like communication," the call succeeds in cutting through the patterns of shared meaning and in summoning Dasein to "the reticence of itself." "'Nothing' gets called to this Self, but it has been summoned to itself—that is, to its ownmost potentiality-for-Being" (318). Hence, authentic realization, or resoluteness, develops by means of an opening to a possibility that cannot be mapped onto the public realm of the "they," a possibility not structured as a "something." Dasein can raise the possibility of being its own self by embracing the meaning of that which is always covered up by "*some*thing": that is, it allows nothing—or the nothing—to become the basis of its own meaningfulness. Accordingly, as the call of conscience penetrates the form of content, "it dispenses with any kind of utterance . . . [and] does not put itself into words at all. . . . *Conscience discourses solely and constantly in the mode of keeping silent*" (318). Consequently, in *Being and Time* everydayness seems to allow, in the end, for only two mutually exclusive forms of relation between ordinary language and the self: being in language and ultimately losing one's self or being one's self in opposition to the rule of everyday language. It follows that the fundamental split between authentic and inauthentic existence—between the ontological and the ontic—is ultimately a dichotomy between intelligibity and the experience of anxiety—facing meaning or facing the nothing—between language and silence.

4. The Aesthetic Elision of the Personal

The conceptualization of language radically changes in Heidegger's later work and the dichotomy discussed above loses its dominance. With the revision of the ontological project language is granted a completely new status. While in *Being and Time* Dasein's reality must serve as the means for philosophically accessing the question of Being, Heidegger now proceeded by bracketing the horizon of daily existence. In so doing he seeks to allow Being to resonate in the proximity of a thinking through the more primordial grid of the poetic.

This can be put another way. The philosophical dialogue with Being in Heidegger's later thought is no longer guided by the nothing that echoes in the silent call of conscience. Rather, the call of language itself is now dominant. That is the original speaking of language in which we are witness to the incarnation of Being in the figure of poetic meaning. This, however, is a rare event since we are typically so radically cut off from the speaking of language. Our distance from the essential grounds of language—and thus from the "neighborhood," as Heidegger puts it, in which thinking and Being reside together—stems from the way we usually go about language: on the one hand, in our common absorption in ordinary use or in the praxis of having a language and, on the other hand, in how we characteristically reflect on language theoretically.

And so, despite his reconceptualization of the being of language and the reassignment of language to an alternative place in his ontology, Heidegger's later turn toward language takes place within a space still dominated, as in *Being and Time*, by the opposition between everydayness and Being, between ordinary language and truth. Even when he embraces language philosophically, the ordinary continues to haunt Heidegger as the enemy of any genuine dialogue with (the being of) language.

"At whatever time and in whatever way we speak a language, language itself never has the floor." Moreover, everyday use is not an external condition of language but, as we noted in looking at the structure of *das Man*, is its very condition of possibility. "Only because in everyday speaking language does not bring itself to language but holds back, are we able simply to go ahead and speak a language, and so to deal with something and negotiate something by speaking."[4] Everyday use not only hides the being of language. It provides a form of concealment that is a necessary condition for maintaining our language routines. Speaking a language is an activity based on the suppression of the very form of language, the form that everything must assume in opening itself to meaning. Language cannot function as it usually does unless it systematically makes way—surrenders itself—to those things, facts, and events of which it is about. We language users, that is, must systematically forget the frame (or form) through which the meaningfulness of the world appears to us.

Language, in other words, "belongs to the nearest neighborhood of man's being."[5] And it is precisely because of this proximity that we ordinarily lose sight of the being of language. The ordinary is a condition of intelligibility constituted by the form of an alienating closeness. This proximity distances us from the being of language, a distance that dominates us in the form of nearness. The ordinary—or everydayness—is the domain in which we encounter meaning through language's complete availability. Language is constantly at our service. It is there for us to use. But, in using language (or, better, in using it up), our absorption in its practical availability conceals its presence as language: it conceals the being of language. It conceals the nature of that original movement by which the intelligible is brought into the open. This is the opening that allows meaning to appear in the first place or, as Heidegger calls it, allows "the speaking of language."

Furthermore, the condition of being severed from this original speaking is not only characteristic of our practical everyday activity. The elision of the being of language not only regulates the appearance of meaning in daily interactions. It also constitutes the basis for our theoretical encounter with the phenomenon. That is, our absorption in the pragmatic typically gives rise to forms of theoretical reflection that, in searching for an objective standpoint, take their leave from the ordinary while remaining committed to—and so inevitably reproducing—the standard of availability inherent in our everyday instrumental relationship to language. In other words, the construction of language as a theoretical subject matter rests on the objectification of those instrumental patterns of use through which we ordinarily, and unreflectively, relate to language. Instead of liberating us from those patterns that conceal the presence of language as language, theoretical reflection generates an objective reproduction of those patterns of deafness and then makes them the basis for our understanding of language.[6]

Our relationship with language is thus, according to Heidegger, caught between the pragmatic form of instrumentality and the theoretical form of the propositional. Language is in both cases enslaved, its essence forgotten. While being regularly subjected to the ways we use up language for our daily communication, language is enslaved once more by theoretical reflection that is unable to recognize the alienated character of everyday language and consequently can only reproduce it in objectified form. The clearest sign of this uncritical reproduction of language's cluelessness is, according to Heidegger, the celebration of information—of the propositional—as language's ultimate standard.[7]

For Heidegger, then, the possibility of freeing language from this double grip and releasing it to its own being necessarily depends on a transformation not only in our understanding but also, more important, in our experience of language. The call for such a transformation is repeated again and again in Heidegger's later work and becomes a central theme in his writing on language. Heidegger opens "The Nature of Language," for example, by announcing his explicit intention "to bring us face to face with a possibility of undergoing an experience with language."

> To undergo an experience with something—be it a thing, a person, or a god—means that this something befalls us, strikes us, comes over us, overwhelms, and transforms us.[8]

The transformative experience by which Heidegger seeks to approach language and to ground a new understanding of the appearance of meaning is twofold. On the one hand, it consists of a radical turning away from the common sphere of intelligibility— a magnetic field— dominated by the mirroring poles of the pragmatic and the propositional.[9] At the same time, it consists of a deliberate turn toward the poetic, which Heidegger understands as the original source and the purest manifestation of meaningfulness as such.[10] The turn to the poetic, i.e., the shift by which the poetic becomes the grounds of our experience of language, is thus meant to open the possibility of reflecting on "language *qua* language," of speaking (philosophically) of "speech *qua* speech." From a different perspective, it is meant to allow "language itself [to] bring itself to language,"[11] to open the possibility through which "language . . . delivered into its own freedom, can be concerned solely with itself."[12]

We cannot really come to terms with Heidegger's understanding of the poetic unless we examine how he reads poetry. This will not be done here, for the novelty of Heidegger's aesthetic insight is of less importance to the present project. Heidegger's shift to the poetic concerns us, rather, because of what it excludes. There is a lesson to be learned from what Heidegger's aesthetic position structurally effaces. And, yes, it effaces the personal. To put this schematically, we may say that the very gesture of delivering language "into its own freedom" severs the phenomenon, almost by definition, from its roots in the speaking individual, in the breath of his mouth, her voice, or the hand that writes. The same Heideggerian gesture that releases the intelligible from its captivity in the domain of everyday use, from its submission to daily human concerns, also leaves language bereft of any trace of the singular individual whose body allows language to resonate in the first place. In retrieving language's original grounds in the purity of speech—in "what is spoken purely"—Heidegger ends up privileging a domain of intelligibility that is purged of all signs of the individual's attachment to language. Heidegger wishes to recollect language onto itself and in so doing leave behind its cognitive, pragmatic, communicative, and expressive functions. But the poetic vision of the origins of language is so sweeping that it ineluctably deprives the phenomenon of language of its whole human physiognomy. Hence, in construing the poetic without the concreteness of individuals, Heidegger makes no distinctions between persons who on occasion use and manipulate language (as one employs a tool) and those who, in speaking, give voice to their intimate rapport with language, who put themselves into the hands of language, and who depend on language as one depends on friends. Heidegger's rejection of individuality is wholesale. In turning to analyze Trakl's poem, "Winter Evening," for example, Heidegger notes the fact that "the poem was written by Georg Trakl" and then immediately qualifies his remark in the following way: "Who the author is remains unimportant here, as with every other masterful poem. The mastery consists precisely in this, that the poem can deny the poet's person and name."[13] For Heidegger, this qualification is not simply meant to suggest that as readers of poetry we must be aware of "the intentional fallacy." Heidegger is not only asking that we bracket certain facts about the author (e.g., biography, intention, etc.), facts that could interfere with the unfolding of meaning in the singular work. What he does, rather, is negate, en bloc, the whole structure of human expressivity, presupposing that structure to be completely homogeneous. Thus, he not only dismisses certain facts about the poem's author but denies the poem its birthplace in the words, the expressive act, of a singular individual. For Heidegger, genuine poetic language is a language purged from the individual presence of its speakers. And this, as suggested, is not the result of any coincidental neglect or failure, but, rather, the outcome of a vision of a primordial intelligibility that cannot ever be a home to the individual because it already is "the house of Being."

5. Van Gogh's Shoes

An illuminating case study for exploring how and why Heidegger's aesthetic turn leads to the effacement of the personal is Heidegger's treatment of a van Gogh painting of shoes in "The Origin of the Work of Art." Van Gogh's painting, which, according to Heidegger, depicts a pair of peasant shoes, not only serves as one of Heidegger's central examples of an artwork but moreover functions as a leitmotif that enables him to develop his key notions of "earth" and "world" in a concrete manner. Heidegger writes,

> From the dark opening of the worn insides of the shoes the toilsome tread of the worker stares forth. In the stiffly rugged heaviness of the shoes there is the accumulated tenacity of her slow trudge through the far-spreading and ever-uniform furrows of the field swept by the raw wind. On the leather lie the dampness and richness of the soil. Under the soles slides the loneliness of the field-path as evening falls. In the shoes vibrates the silent call of the earth, its quiet gift of the ripening rain and its unexplained self-refusal in the fallow desolation of the wintry field. This equipment is pervaded by uncomplaining anxiety as to the certainty of bread, the wordless joy of having once more withstood want, the trembling before the impending childbed and shivering at the surrounding menace of death. This equipment belongs to the *earth,* and it is protected in the *world* of the peasant woman. From out of this protected belonging the equipment itself arises to its resting-within-itself.[14]

While first serving as the means for elaborating the relation between "earth" and "world," the van Gogh painting continues to figure again and again in Heidegger's general discussion of the art work, eventually serving as the epitome of Heidegger's conception of art as the occurrence of truth. More specifically, it is in the context of Heidegger's discussion of "equipmentality" or "instrumentality" that the specificity of the painting becomes significant. For Heidegger, van Gogh's painting shows how a work of art can release us from the captivating structure of ordinary intelligibility and bring us face to face with the poetic unfolding of Being. In contrast to the quest for Being in *Being and Time*, Heidegger's aesthetic path does not require the evacuation of the intelligible. Rather, it proceeds as a restoration of the primordial intelligibility that lies hidden and mute within, and is perhaps even mutilated by, the equipmental form of the appearance of meaning in everydayness. The being of shoes, like that of language, is both constituted and concealed by the prism of use. We cannot see shoes without having their instrumental structure pervade our perception. That is, for the peasant woman, the shoes are precisely what she wears every day. Yet, this means that she can only encounter them through the prism of ordinary use, without having access to the global condition of equipmentality—i.e., her captivity in the pragmatic—that creates the horizons of ordinary meaning in the first place. And so, while the meaningfulness of actual shoes manifests our human confinement to a world whose horizons are essentially equipmental, van Gogh's painted shoes, "the empty, unused shoes as they merely stand there in the picture" (33), open up the possibility of experiencing the intelligible in a manner that is no longer imprisoned by that pragmatic standard. The painting offers a perspectival shift through which the inner form of the equipmental can be revealed and so be transcended.

> The equipmental character of equipment was discovered. But how? Not by a description and explanation of a pair of shoes actually present; not by a report about the process of making shoes; and also not by the observation of the actual use of shoes occurring here and there; but only by bringing ourselves before Van Gogh's painting. This painting spoke. In the vicinity of the work we were suddenly somewhere else than we usually tend to be. The art work let us know what the shoes are in truth. *(35)*

Furthermore, van Gogh's painting not only serves Heidegger by revealing how the equipmental form of everydayness obscures the being of entities but also by exemplifying how a work of art enacts truth. "Van Gogh's painting is the disclosure of what the equipment, the pear of peasant shoes, is in truth. This entity emerges into the unconcealedness of its being. The Greeks called the unconcealedness of beings *aletheia*" (36). For Heidegger, in other words, the painting becomes an epitome of his conception of art as the occurrence of truth: "Truth happens in the van Gogh painting" (56). And "the reference to van Gogh's picture" is understood as an attempt "to point to this happening" and, "with regard to it," give rise to "the question as to what truth is and how truth can happen" (41).

The poetic, according to Heidegger, is an event that releases the space of human intelligibility from the mirroring constraints of both the pragmatic and the propositional. The work of the artwork is thus found in the opening of a possibility of meaningfulness, a path for thinking, that is no longer dominated by functionality or by the propositional standard of representation. The other side of this is that van Gogh's painting cannot be understood in terms of its representational content. Instead, it should be encountered within the horizons of that event of unconcealment of which we ourselves would be part if we succeed in opening for the painting the possibility of its own communicability.

Hence, Heidegger's aesthetic gesture toward the emancipation of thinking from its captivity in the ordinary goes hand in hand with his insistence on the possibility of allowing the painting to open up and uphold forth its "simple *factum est*" (65). Heidegger's philosophical principle of "letting be" issues from an understanding of the need to overcome the structural condition or the predicament of a thinking that cannot open up to what it posits as its object without eliding it as a thing. That is, the possibility of letting the thing be is the mark of an alternative mode of thinking that seeks to release itself from this pathology: a mode of thinking that liberates itself in setting free the being of that which it encounters. Heidegger understands the encounter—his own philosophical encounter—with van Gogh's painting in this manner. The painting offers itself only to the kind of thinking whose openness is not based on appropriation. The encounter with this kind of thinking (e.g., Heidegger's own thinking) allows the painting to open up as it never could or did under the reign of traditional propositional thinking. The painting has been allowed to speak and, as Heidegger tells us, "this painting spoke" (35).

But what are the philosophical consequences of this epiphany? What is the price to be paid for the emancipation of the artwork from its factual or representational underpinnings? My answer is already clear: despite its appeal, Heidegger's rhetoric of "letting be" remains removed and foreign to the claims of the personal that, in essence, lives in the heart of our human attachment to content and cannot be encountered if we understand content only as a limiting factor. In many ways this is how I read the motivation behind Meyer Schapiro's famous attack, or "complaint," against Heidegger's metaphysical appropriation of van Gogh's painting.

In "The Still Life as a Personal Object: Note on Heidegger and van Gogh," art historian Meyer Schapiro has argued that Heidegger's discussion of van Gogh's painting of a pair of peasant shoes rests on a crude misidentification of the painting's reference, one that necessarily undermines Heidegger metaphysical conception of art. Schapiro, however, is wholly uninterested in understanding the metaphysics he criticizes. What concerns Schapiro is the painting itself. And since Heidegger "does not identify the picture he has in mind," the argument, according to Schapiro, depends on a reference that is too vague and obscure to make any real point. Moreover, as Schapiro has culled additional details concerning the painting to which Heidegger refers, his objection only intensifies. Schapiro argues that the philosopher's exemplification process is inconsequential since the specific example he considers does not actually exist. Schapiro contends, and moves to demonstrate, that Heidegger has failed to identify the reference for the depicted shoes because the shoes painted by van Gogh are not artifacts of peasant life. They are, in fact, the artist's own shoes—"the artist by that time a man of the town and the city"—and as such they carry a specific biographical significance. "Alas for him," Schapiro writes, "the philosopher has deceived himself."

[He] has retained from the encounter with Van Gogh's canvas a moving set of associations with peasants and the soil which are not sustained by the picture itself. They are grounded rather in his social outlook with its heavy pathos of the primordial and earthy. He has indeed "imagined everything and projected it into the painting." He has experienced both too little and too much in his contact with the work.[15]

But even if Heidegger has mistaken the actual reference of the shoes, is this relevant to the validity of his aesthetic position? Or, as W. J. T. Mitchell sarcastically asks, "Does Schapiro believe that Heidegger's 'error' about van Gogh's shoes invalidates his more general philosophical arguments about the nature of art?"[16]

Since its publication in 1968, Schapiro's attack on Heidegger has become a well-known "episode" (principally due to the response it provoked from Jacques Derrida), and a common point of reference for theory. At the same time, keeping with Derrida's glib "Restitutions," the relevance of this episode to central issues in the contemporary debate has never actually been explored.[17] Schapiro's criticism has had no impact on our understanding of the relation between philosophy and art history, nor on our understanding of Heidegger's philosophy of art. This is primarily because the "sheer" historicism of Schapiro's note has rendered his text irrelevant to the philosophical, or theoretical, language game. The facts that concern the art historian have been seen as lacking any importance to philosophical reflection on art and are often taken as testimony to the art historian's "unwillingness to engage in the theory and philosophy of art."[18] Hence, for, W. J. T. Mitchell, Schapiro's "notorious Note" is "one of the most depressing episodes in art history's continued failure to engage with theory and philosophy in the twentieth century."

In my view, however, the polemic between Schapiro and Heidegger is particularly relevant to our discussion. Schapiro's critique may indeed be ultimately ineffective. Yet, it is precisely its apparent failure that teaches us something important about the philosophical invulnerability that is characteristic of Heidegger's text. That is, in his nonphilosophical insistence on the facts of van Gogh's painting, Schapiro can help us shed valuable light on a vulnerable dimension of meaning that Heidegger effaces by bracketing ordinary human facts. However, to begin with, we need to notice that the presuppositions that inform Schapiro's critique of Heidegger are grounded in a positivistic, albeit Marxist, perspective. For Schapiro, Heidegger's text necessarily operates as one of two mutually exclusive possibilities: either Heidegger's philosophy is a scientific theory (whose concepts are legitimately formed and whose statements meet strict criteria of factual validity) or it is an expressive pseudo theory that, despite its "strong conviction," must ultimately be meaningless. For Schapiro, Heidegger's use of a van Gogh painting can either support the "theoretical idea" of the "metaphysical power of art" or fail to do so. And since the example Heidegger uses is factually flawed, it "does not support that idea."

Schapiro thus treats Heidegger as if he were a philosopher who simply fails to meet the positivist's criteria of meaning, whereas Heidegger is a thinker who explicitly labors to problematize the philosophical framework underlying such criteria of meaning. In other words, Schapiro reads Heidegger without recognizing that the point of the latter's aesthetics is to open up a new possibility for reflection, a possibility no longer governed by and providing an alternative to a propositional (as well as to a pragmatic) conception of meaning and truth.

Nevertheless, it seems to me that, despite his misreading of Heidegger, Schapiro's critique contains an important lesson, one whose significance rests in the fact that the shoes van Gogh decided to paint are not, after all, the shoes of a peasant woman. We need to come to terms with this factual point because its significance lies beyond the merely factual. What is it then that gets lost in the factual mistake Heidegger makes, and why is it philosophically important?

In answering this question, we first need to notice that Heidegger's position cannot at all be undermined by the factual identity of the shoes because the identity of the shoes is not critical to what he wants to say. This is clearly demonstrated once we notice that the van Gogh example is essentially replaceable. Heidegger could have, in principle, accommodated Schapiro's alternative description of the shoes without sacrificing the crux of his argument. While only slightly altering his rhetoric, Heidegger would have no problem developing his line of thought by adopting as an example a painting that depicted the painter's city shoes. On the other hand, had he wanted to retain the image of the peasantry, Heidegger could have also reestablished his argument with a more correct example, that is, a painting by van Gogh or by someone else that actually depicts a pair of peasant shoes.

One may go further and claim that Schapiro's criticism does not, and cannot, undermine Heidegger's argument because the actual painting, the painting in its specificity, does not really matter to Heidegger's case. The van Gogh example functions in calling to mind our more general, or generic, experience as viewers of art. Since the disclosure of the truth concerning equipment depends on turning from one's ordinary view of things to an experience of looking at pictures of a certain sort (paintings depicting day-to-day objects), all that is needed is an example that brings about, or carries within itself, the proper analogical contexts: a tension between the ordinary object and its visual representation that opens a new vantage for seeing the equipmental dimension of our human situatedness.

This implies that for Heidegger the van Gogh painting is no more than a means of exemplification. It is a mere illustration—expendable, subsidiary—of a self-sufficient, self-generating line of thought. Put differently, it seems that, for Heidegger, the van Gogh painting plays a completely heuristic role. Heidegger uses the artwork without any concern for it in and of itself. He is ultimately uninterested in attending to how the specificity of the painting relates to the possibility of disclosure that does concern him. He exchanges the painting's singularity for what he understands to be the artwork's general ability to subvert the equipmental, an ability that seems to rest on the most typical, even banal, ways in which we engage art. Thus, despite the rhetoric of liberating art from its traditionally subordinate role, art's ascension to an apparently new status in "The Origin of the Work of Art" is only made possible by the instrumental form of "in-order-to." Art exists only in the form of a service. A service to whom? To philosophy. In this respect, we need to note that Heidegger's attitude toward the thing as art is based on a form of blindness analogous to that which he criticizes. Just as someone can be so lost in the equipment one uses that it is not seen as equipment, Heidegger's philosophy of art promotes an absorption that obscures the singular presence of the thing as art. Hence, although a specific factual inaccuracy cannot dismantle Heidegger's position, we may now see that the problematic nature of Heidegger's treatment of van Gogh's painting does not derive at all from the destructive threat of facts. Rather, it issues from the inability of the facts to matter at all. Heidegger's conception of the artwork is disconcerting not because it can be refuted by certain factual evidence but because his indifference toward the facts carries absolutely no implications for the validity of his thinking. In other words, the philosophical relevance of Schapiro's criticism does not lie in its ability to expose the vulnerability of Heidegger's thinking, but, paradoxically, the invulnerability of that thinking. Schapiro's criticism becomes philosophically significant when it allows us to see that Heidegger's thinking remains completely unaffected by and immune to the pleas of the examples it employs.

Heidegger's treatment of van Gogh's painting is not the case of a philosopher who has made a simple perceptual mistake or who misidentified or misinterpreted what he saw in a painting. Heidegger, rather, is a philosopher who takes for granted that what appears in a painting conforms to what he thinks of the painting. He is a philosopher whose factual error is the outcome, and in this sense a symptom, of a philosophical indifference toward the claims of the concrete. This indifference, or neglectfulness, should be understood within the general context of Heidegger's bias against the visual, one that already finds its clearest expression in *Being and Time*'s conceptualization of sight as a superficial aspect of our being, i.e., as one of the characteristic features of our fallenness or inauthentic existence.[19] But, for our purposes, however, what specifically matters is the connection between Heidegger's predisposition toward the visually concrete and the kind of textuality within which he operates.

For Heidegger, the appearance of the visual is not in itself an origin of meaning toward which the text must make an effort to turn, reach out, or break open. On the contrary, for Heidegger, the particularity of the visual—its unique presence as something which is seen—has no significance beyond what already belongs to the domain of the text. In Heidegger's text, in other words, the visual is allowed to appear only in the form of meanings that language already inhabits, meanings that are in principle already to be found within the space of the text. The reconstruction of the visual in "The Origin of the Work of Art" is carried out without leaving any trace of resistance, residue, or difference. For Heidegger, a verbal description of the painting indeed suffices, and it suffices in the sense that nothing more is needed—that the text in itself is complete enough—for a meaningful engagement with the painting's visuality. It is also then not surprising that Heidegger sees no real need for providing a specific reference to, or even a reproduction of, the painting that ostensibly concerns him. And yet, what is missing in Heidegger's text is not a specific pictorial supplement, a visual aid, but a form of sensitivity without which philosophy cannot meet the visual. In other words, Heidegger's error is, in my view, a cause for concern because it is a symptom of a philosophy, or of a form of reflection that engages with—and attempts to think about—the visual without actually looking.[20]

Heidegger allows van Gogh's painting to assume its own power to speak: "This painting spoke." But, where and how does this happen? In a philosopher's text. It is the philosophical text that functions here as the grounds for the self-disclosure of the work of art. Moreover, the whole framing of this event already presupposes a particular, a pregiven, understanding of the painting's conditions of speech. According to this understanding, the painting is essentially a mute object whose communicability depends on those singular moments of oracular grace that are inspired by the guidance of the philosopher.[21] What may thus easily hide in the gesture of emancipating the painting's speech is a patronizing attitude that imposes on the communicability of the painting the confines of a philosophical event. To put this differently, we may say that the philosophical setting that supposedly allows the painting to speak does not make room for the ways in which the painting is always already in the midst of speaking. That is, when the philosophical gesture of emancipation becomes the center of the encounter with a painting, it typically turns a blind eye to the primacy of the painting's speech, to the unique status of the painting as the ultimate origin of its own speech. This gesture typically suppresses the genuine otherness of the painting's speech, effacing the possibility of a speech that is not born, and does not necessarily develop, within the space of philosophy.

What I am suggesting is that in his opposition to the reification of the phenomenon of meaning, Heidegger's thematics of "letting be" also opens a dangerous philosophical pitfall hard to resist and into which Heidegger himself ultimately stumbles. This is the allure of a thinking that fully sustains itself from within—the philosophical temptation to totalize the space, or the affect, of thought. In presupposing such a totality of thinking, Heidegger is consequently closed to forms of intelligibility whose origin is not, at bottom, philosophical. This means that he can only engage with meanings or forms of presence that are already a part of and assimilated into his space of discourse. More specifically, I believe that Heidegger's textuality—characterized by its affect of totality, its forgetfulness of its limitations and even of the fact that it has limits—prevents the possibility of philosophically encountering the nonphilosophical voice of van Gogh's painting on the basis of a dialogue or a conversation. This would be a conversation between two forms of speech or meaningfulness—in this case, the textual and the visual—that are truly different, that do not share the same origin, and that do not necessarily coincide. To say this is very close to saying that Heidegger's later thinking makes no room for listening to the concrete alterity always present in the speech of the other.

6. Sabina's Hat

The structure of everydayness is not our prison. We become prisoners of the ordinary only once we internalize the opposition between our freedom and certain dominant structures of the everyday. The idea that everydayness is a form of captivity is often more captivating than the average forms of everydayness. This can be seen in the encounter with the personal that allows existence to show itself in the midst of the averageness of the everyday. In order to encounter meaning free from the rule of the average, we need neither to transcend the ordinary object nor to radically transform it, as Meret Oppenheim, for example, does—using a tea cup—in her *Luncheon in Fur*. There is another way: to develop an attentive ear for the delicate resonance of the creative potential—the call of freedom—contained in the most ordinary of objects.

Unlike Heidegger, for whom van Gogh's painted shoes serve as means for releasing the ordinary object from its equipmental form, what concerns us here is the need to recognize that our ordinary relationship to shoes is never really dominated by the pragmatic in the first place. We need to see, for example, that it is only because the form of equipment did not regulate van Gogh's attachment to his shoes that he turned them into the subject of his painting. In other words, van Gogh's painting not only opens up a unique possibility for releasing the ordinary object (a pair of shoes) from its captivity in the pragmatic. It reveals, most of all, how the pragmatic structures of the ordinary can never fully dominate the meaningfulness of ordinary objects, how the meaningfulness of an ordinary pair of shoes is never really that ordinary. In this sense, we may note again how Heidegger's misidentification of the painted shoes matches his blindness toward forms of personal attachment that are irreducible to the averageness of *das Man*.

Hence, to elaborate further on what it means for an ordinary object to appear as a personal object, let us take another example. This time, rather than shoes, we will examine a hat, a bowler hat, "the kind of hat—black, hard, round— . . . that Chaplin wore."[22] The hat that concerns us belongs to Sabina, one of the protagonists of Kundera's *The Unbearable Lightness of Being*. Sabina is a Czech painter who emigrates to Geneva after the Russian invasion of her country. The bowler hat, which once belonged to her grandfather, a mayor in Bohemia, and was one of the few possessions she took with her from Prague, is placed on a wig stand alongside a mirror in her Geneva studio. This bowler hat is a completely ordinary, generic, and functional object, and yet it well exemplifies how any attempt to fit it into, or read it according to, a pragmatic matrix such as Heidegger's would destroy its meaningfulness.

Sabina's hat appears in various places in the novel. The specific episode that concerns us here is part of a chapter entitled "Words Misunderstood" that describes the nature of the relationship between Sabina and Franz, her lover. Franz is a successful university professor whose guilt feelings toward his wife do not permit him to have sex with Sabina in Geneva itself, but only in more remote places. This means that whenever Franz visits Sabina in her studio it is "only as a friend, never as a lover." From a slightly different perspective this means that, since the beginning of his affair with Sabina, Franz has been traveling extensively to scientific conferences.

This time he drops by to invite Sabina to travel with him to a conference in Palermo. "How would you like to go to Palermo ten days from now?" he asks. But Sabina, who is described as working on a canvass, does not appear to be in the mood for traveling. "I prefer Geneva," she answers. The two continue to discuss the issue when, "with a curious nonchalance, as if completely unaware of Franz's presence," Sabina suddenly takes off her blouse. The episode develops as follows:

> Standing there in her skirt and bra, she suddenly . . . fixed Franz with a long stare. That stare bewildered him; he could not understand it. . . . It had nothing in common with the looks and gestures that usually preceded their lovemaking. It was neither provocative nor flirtatious, simply interrogative. The problem was, Franz had not the slightest notion what it was asking. Next she stepped out of her skirt and, taking Franz by the hand, turned him in the direction of a large mirror propped against the wall. Without letting go of his hand, she looked into the mirror with the same long questioning stare, training it first on herself, then on him. Near the mirror stood a wig stand with an old black bowler hat on it. She bent over, picked up the hat, and put it on her head. The image in the mirror was instantaneously transformed: suddenly it was a woman in her undergarment, a beautiful, distant, indifferent woman with a terribly out-of-place bowler hat on her head, holding the hand of a man in a grey suit and tie. Again he had to smile at how poorly he understood his mistress.

When she took her clothes off, it wasn't so much erotic provocation as an odd little caper, a happening *a deux*. His smile beamed understanding and consent. He waited for his mistress to respond in kind, but she did not. Without letting go of his hand, she stood staring into the mirror, first at herself, then at him. The time for the happening has come and gone. Franz was beginning to feel that the caper . . . had dragged on too long. So he gently took the brim of the bowler hat between two fingers, lifted it off Sabina's head with a smile, and laid it back on the wig stand. It was as though he were erasing the moustache a naughty child had drawn on a picture of the Virgin Mary. For several more seconds she remained motionless, staring at herself in the mirror. Then Franz covered her with tender kisses and asked her once more to go with him in ten days to Palermo. This time she said yes unquestionably, and he left. He was in excellent mood again. Geneva, which he has cursed all his life as the metropolis of boredom, now seemed beautiful and full of adventure. *(82)*

Despite the fact that the scene ends in positive agreement (Sabina accedes to Franz's request and makes him happy), it presents at its core a failure of understanding. Sabina's gestures remain illegible and impenetrable to Franz, just like the opacity of her bowler hat, which is a blind spot in his perception of her. The scene that begins with the unexpected gesture of Sabina's undressing reaches its climax when, looking at and through the mirror, Sabina puts on her bowler hat. The scene ends once Franz imposes closure on the situation. Sabina's gestures opens up to meaning in two interrelated ways. On the one hand, there is the revelation, or exposure, of her naked body, i.e., an act of disclosure. On the other hand, there is a questioning, or a presentation of a question. Sabina's self-disclosure, in other words, opens up in the form of a question. This question remains unpronounced and unanswered but it is constantly manifested in the interrogative gaze she fixes on Franz and, more generally, in the reflective character of the entire event occurring in the presence of a mirror. Sabina's image, gaze, and action are reflected in the mirror. But her question is not self-reflexive. Nor is it meant for an indefinite audience. We may say, rather, that Sabina poses herself as a question to Franz. She is not just interested in the mere echoing of her question but in opening herself up as a question to the particular person who looks at her. The question she asks is meant for Franz and for Franz only. Its meaningfulness is constituted by the horizon of Franz's presence.

We shall return to Sabina's question. First, however, let us note that this scene contains yet another dimension. This dimension is born of the intersection between Sabina's self-disclosure and her questioning. It is manifest in the gesture of wearing the bowler hat. Kundera describes this gesture as transformative—"the image in the mirror was instantaneously transformed"—but we may go further and say that it is creative. That is, what appears between Sabina's self-disclosure and her questioning is her creativity. The mirror replaces Sabina's canvas in this scene, but her artistic position in relation to meaning has not changed. Her creativity is not confined to the canvas but is integral, as marked by her use of the bowler, to her orientation toward the everyday. For Franz, however, the meaning of Sabina's behavior remains uncharted. He is baffled by the situation, one that seems to defy any familiar classification. In particular, he cannot make sense of the manner in which the bowler hat has come into focus. He does not understand what Sabina is trying to communicate in putting the old hat on. For a passing moment Franz seems close to losing his well-tempered balance, but because he is a clever and kind person, and because he genuinely cares about Sabina, he does not allow his uncertainty and momentary insecurity to accentuate the gap that opened between them. On the contrary, he pushes his way back to a mutual understanding with Sabina. Franz literally removes the obstacle that caused their rift and puts the bowler hat away. He covers her (uncovered) body with kisses and finally returns to the initial conversation they had started, thus replacing Sabina's question (that he could not understand and that was an intrinsically open question) with a clear-cut, yes-or-no question. Franz "asked her once more to go with him in ten days to Palermo. This time she said yes unquestionably, and he left."

While Franz's satisfaction allows him to immediately forget the bowler hat, and so erase all traces of the rupture in his understanding of Sabina, Sabina, alone again in her studio, returns to the mirror and replaces the hat back on her head. From a Heideggerian perspective, a bowler hat, like a pair of peasant shoes, is a prototypical example of the generic, essentially anonymous, and instrumental form of everyday objects. However, for Sabina, this ordinary, familiar object is far from being anything resembling Heideggerian equipment. Is this so simply because of the outdated quality of the bowler? No. It is so, rather, because this object embodies—it appears through—a netting of personal and biographical significations that cannot be reduced to the pragmatic. Constituted by its unique "mixing [of] memory and desire" (to borrow from T. S. Eliot), the complicated presence of the bowler hat would be completely lost if condensed into the narrow confines of the equipmental. The meaningfulness of the hat rests on Sabina's peculiar attachment to it. This attachment has nothing in common with a generic instrumental relationship to an object. First of all, the hat "has" a story. Through this story it becomes a meaningful part of Sabina's world.

> First, it was a vague reminder of a forgotten grandfather, the mayor of a small Bohemian town during the nineteenth century. Second, it was a memento of her father. After the funeral her brother appropriated all their parents' property, and she, refusing out of sovereign contempt to fight for her rights, announced sarcastically that she was taking the bowler hat as her sole inheritance. Third, it was a prop for her lover games with Tomas. Fourth, it was a sign of her originality, which she consciously cultivated. She could not take much with her when she emigrated and taking this bulky, impractical thing meant giving up other, more practical ones. Fifth, now that she was abroad it was a sentimental object. *(84)*

The hat, however, is not just a sign for distinctive moments in the trajectory of Sabina's life. According to Kundera,

> the bowler hat was a motif in the musical composition that was Sabina's life. It returned again and again, each time with a different meaning, and all the meanings flowed through the bowler hat like water through a riverbed. I might call it Heraclitus' . . . riverbed: the bowler hat was a bed through which each time Sabina saw another

river flow, another semantic river. Each time the same object would give rise to a new meaning, though all former meanings would resonate (like an echo, like a parade of echoes) together with the new one. Each new experience would resound, each time enriching the harmony. *(84)*

Sabina's hat speaks to her in various voices. It is suffused with the presence of her father, her childhood, her country, her language, her history, her relation to men, her singular love for Tomas, the failure of this love, her choices, fantasies, dreams, hopes, independence, pride, loneliness, etc. But what makes the hat so significant, according to Kundera, is not its embodiment of any given set of determinate meanings. Its significance arises, rather, from the very manner in which the hat opens up, through time, the flow and adumbration of ever new meanings for Sabina. For Kundera, alongside the shared and average forms of semantically structured meanings, there is a more subtle flow of meaning that is more difficult to detect: "the semantic susurrus of the river flowing through them" (84). This continuous murmuring of meaning, one that Franz fails to hear, marks the bowler hat's roots in the temporality of Sabina's world. Sabina's hat is not a fully constituted object. It does not exist in any final way, nor is its meaningfulness exhausted by the facts that are true about it. Instead, the bowler hat is an object genuinely belonging to Sabina's present. Its meaningfulness unfolds in the tension—the mutual interplay—between the heaviness of the past and the openness of an uncharted future. Alternatively, we can say that the bowler hat not only enfolds a story with which Franz is unacquainted but that it has a life of which Franz is not—and, according to Kundera, cannot be—a part.

Kundera's metaphor in speaking here of a person's life is that of a "musical composition."

> While people are fairly young and the musical composition of their life is still in its opening bars, they can go about writing it together and exchange motifs. . . . But if they meet when they are older, like Franz and Sabina, their musical compositions are more or less com-

plete, and every motif, every object, every word means something different to each of them. *(85)*

That is to say, despite their mutual intimacy, a permanent unbridgeable "abyss separating Sabina and Franz" is always in existence. And so, "when she put on the bowler hat in his presence, Franz felt uncomfortable, as if someone had spoken to him in a language he did not know. It was neither obscene nor sentimental, merely an incomprehensible gesture. What made him feel uncomfortable was its very lack of meaning" (85).

Kundera describes Sabina's hat as the semantic river Franz can never cross. His picture shows us that the two conditions of affectionately sharing a world with another person and of being worlds apart from that person are not mutually exclusive. Moreover, Kundera reveals to us here how the depth of misunderstanding is not always definite or determinate: the significant gaps in our understanding of others are not at all informational in character. Accordingly, even if Franz could have obtained all the relevant information about Sabina's hat he would still remain deaf to those "semantic susurrus" in which the private meaning of Sabina's handling of the hat is embodied.

On this point, however, I think that Kundera's description might be slightly misleading. This is especially so in the comparison he draws between Franz and a person who cannot make sense of a foreign language. Do we really want to say that Sabina has another private language? That is, does Sabina actually speak in two tongues? Does she express a double meaning, one familiar and the other unrevealed? One through a public and the other through an utterly private language? Moreover, would it be right to describe Franz's failure in terms of a simple failure to understand a foreign language? Is this only a cognitive failure? Is it at all a cognitive failure?

Sabina allows meaning to appear in a manner that makes Franz feel a complete outsider. But even if we wish to describe Franz as an outsider in relation to Sabina's meaning, we should, at the same time, notice that what he remains alienated from is not any kind of sealed, exclusive space within which private meanings dwell.

Meaning is in the open. It hides no backrooms with stolen merchandise. No alternative domain of content exists outside of what the public mechanisms of language can express. "Nothing is hidden" (to use a Wittgensteinian phrase). Sabina hides no secret. Consequently, Franz's failure does not lie in a blindness issuing from something that his eyes are not made to see. On the contrary, what elides him is precisely that which is made for his eyes only. Franz looks at Sabina. Her behavior surprises him. Franz's attempt to understand her is the attempt to find a given term, or a general pattern—a concept, a description—that would enable him to determine the meaning of what he sees. He fails. And yet, despite his discontent, he remains entirely committed to the public averageness that guides his understanding of meaning. For him, understanding Sabina can only mean one thing: it means to embrace her intelligibility as—and we go back to Heidegger—"something familiar and accessible to everyone" (*Being and Time*, 165). In this respect, Franz is a good example of a person who completely internalizes and whose experience of meaning wholly depends on the anonymous gaze of everyone as its standard. Franz, in other words, is an exemplary citizen in the dictatorship of *das Man*. (In Kundera's terms, he genuinely belongs to the "metropolis of boredom.")

What Franz cannot see is that meaning has opened up between Sabina and himself in a completely singular way, in a manner that would dissolve immediately if put in terms applicable to everyone. The actuality of Sabina's "speaking" is irreplaceable. It does not adhere to any general form for conveying meaning. Sabina's act cannot be understood, that is, if we are to put ourselves "in her shoes." When she dons the bowler hat no one else can be her. Sabina, in other words, must be listened to as Sabina, or, more specifically, as Sabina speaking to Franz.

We have thus arrived at the personal—the singular presence of a person in everyday meanings. The personal resides in the averageness of everyday intelligibility, and yet it is not, as Heidegger thinks, leveled off by that averageness. However, the appearance of the personal is neither immediate nor secure. In particular, since it is couched in the I-you relationship—since it takes two to tango—the personal quite often remains hidden. As Kundera shows (in his description of Franz), it is easy to efface the personal. But its appearance depends on us: we are responsible for the appearance of the personal. In this respect, we can read Franz's failure to find personal meaning in Sabina's act as an invitation. How could we give a place to the personal in that encounter? How would we respond in place of Franz? What would it mean to listen in a personal way to what Sabina is saying? Is there a particular kind of experience of meaning that underlies the appearance of the personal? What would it mean to encounter the personal?

We may begin answering these questions by thinking again of the musical metaphor—the metaphor of a musical motif—Kundera uses to describe the private, or singular, dimension of meaning. This metaphor, as suggested, calls for understanding the personal in a way not governed by the form of information. Understanding a musical theme does not depend on knowing what the fact of the matter is (which is perhaps why Wittgenstein says that "understanding a sentence is much more akin to understanding a theme in music than one may think").[23] If we extend Kundera's metaphor, we may contend that, in playing her bowler hat motif to Franz, Sabina was not inviting Franz to listen to her music as much as she was inviting him to join in with her and play together. In other words, Franz's failure should not be understood as a failure to construe an accurate factual picture of what Sabina was doing. His failure was not cognitive but artistic or creative. Franz was unable to allow the personal to appear because he was blind to the option of responding creatively to Sabina, because creativity remained foreign to the beat of the heart of his relationship with her.

We could alternatively say that Franz was unable to find (or should we say create?) an answer to that "long questioning stare" through which Sabina showed herself to him. The presence of a question did not escape Franz's attention, but "[he] had not the slightest notion what it was asking." Again, his misunderstanding issued from the presupposition that a legible question must necessarily correspond to a factual answer. As Franz understood the situation, if Sabina was not just being provocative or flirtatious but actually meant to ask him something, then her question must by definition contain a determinate—i.e., a propositional—content, much like his own question, "How would you like to go to Palermo ten days from now?" Recalling our discussion of Kierkegaard and Kafka in chapter 2, we may also recognize Franz to be a person who relates to the structure of language as if it were a given fact, a fact that fully determines the horizons of his freedom in language. That is, Franz subscribes to the familiar patterns of language in a manner that conceals his freedom and thus absolves him of responsibility for realizing that freedom in his daily encounter with Sabina.

Shouldn't we therefore think of his misunderstanding of Sabina as an ethical failure? And how should we understand Sabina? I think that the way Sabina relates to meaning deserves to be called "poetic." Her relation to meaning is poetic, but, at the same time, that relation follows a path whose unfolding is incompatible with the poetic path taken by Heidegger. Is she necessarily more distant than Heidegger from that "original" Greek sense of the term *poiesis*? Sabina shares neither the Heideggerian nostalgia for the lost primordiality of meaning nor the Heideggerian aversion to the ordinary. While for Heidegger "truth is never gathered from objects that are present and ordinary," for Sabina the ordinary is the only place where human truth can appear. While Heidegger sees "everyday language [as] a forgotten and therefore used-up poem, from which there hardly resounds a call any longer," for Sabina the poetic is a manifestation of our freedom in everyday language. Sabina, in other words, is a poet of the everyday.

Within the fixed horizons of his relation to meaning, this was something Franz could not understand. He could not see—and perhaps we should even say that he did not want to see or that he was afraid to acknowlede—that Sabina's treatment of the ordinary issued from her singularity as a person. Sabina did not communicate content. She posited existence. She faced Franz without allowing his expectations—neither the structure of language nor her biography—to determine her meaningfulness. She communicated: "Here I am," "This is I."

This declaration of existence is not, as it might at first seem, an assertion. Sabina did not assert herself but did something radically different. She let her singularity as a person appear. Sabina's "This is I" is not a proposition, for a proposition issues from the dyad man-world. The grounds for her act, in contrast, is the presence of a witness. She does not utter a saying in the face of things, nor offer one resting on the Heideggerian dyad of Being versus man. In contrast to Heidegger's description of the cosmic, limitless echo of the art work—the "painting spoke"—Sabina's speaks to Franz in particular. She spoke to him. And in allowing Franz to become the genuine horizon of her singularity—I can see you. Can you see me?—her saying unfolds as a question. Sabina's "This is I" is not a proposition, neither a statement nor an assertion, but a vulnerable, self-disclosing question. What Sabina asks Franz, and what he refuses to hear is the question: Am I? Is this I? Is this me?

In concluding this chapter, we may say that the ability to hear Sabina's question is a condition for encountering the personal. In order to encounter the personal we need to learn to recognize the singularity of existence in a pair of shoes or in an old hat. That is, we need to learn to listen to the poetic voice of the ordinary, to see how the ordinary is poetic. This is not always a simple thing to do, as should be apparent by now. On the one hand, the poetic has a tendency to direct our thinking to the limits—if not beyond the limits—of the ways we talk to each other. And, thus it turns our philosophical gaze away from the place in which our shoes stand. On the other hand, our ordinary routines with language often seem to lead our philosophical gaze toward forms of communication that hardly leave a trace of the poetic.

Perhaps the best way to end this discussion is by means of a poem that allows us to hear the personal speaking from within the averageness of the everyday. "Pleasures"[24] belongs to Brecht's *Last Poems* (1953–56). Because of the tenderness and intimacy it expresses toward the ordinary, this is the kind of poem that is most likely to escape Heidegger's appreciation.

Pleasures

The first look out of the window in the morning
The old book found again
Enthusiastic faces
Snow, the change of seasons
The newspaper
The dog
Dialectics
Taking showers, swimming
Old music
Comfortable shoes
Taking things in
New music
Writing, planting
Travelling
Singing
Being friendly

5

CHAPTER 5
Language Unframed: Beauty as a Model

We need to think the personal while allowing everyday language to reverberate in our ears. This may be very difficult to do, but it is also simple. It is difficult because the return to ordinary speech is more complicated than it seems or because ordinary speech is not as ordinary as philosophers of language seem to believe. We must recognize, therefore, that ordinary language is not simply equivalent to that sphere of possibilities that a language can, in principle, express in everyday circumstances. That is to say, the logical possibilities open to everyday speech should not be understood, although they often are, as reflective of our actual speech. When a philosopher attends to what we say in language through such instances of speech as "Wulf is a dog," "*That bar* is the standard meter stick," "I met a man I'll call 'Binkley.' Binkley is a mechanic," "The first postmaster general spoke French well," or "Fred says 'the man in the corner with the champagne in his glass is very angry,'"[1] we may note his clear sense of commitment to the colloquial character of daily language. At the same time, we should not conflate the colloquial character of these examples with how we actually talk. Despite their casual appearance, the above examples do not grow out of the situatedness of language in the contingent concreteness of everyday circumstances. They are, rather, read off a ready-made matrix of abstract possibilities that only mirror, and remain external to, the ways we live our lives. In other words, "Wulf is a dog" or "I met a man I'll call Binkley" are sentences that may seem to belong to ordinary language because they are simple and colloquial, because they are sentences we can easily imagine ourselves saying. On a closer look we need to notice that these are, in fact, fabricated examples that relate, if at all, to very specific situations. The situations that make room for this sort of speech—"Wulf is a dog"—either involve peculiar or infantile learning circumstances (What kind of animal is Wulf? Wulf is a dog) or, more probably, issue from philosophy classes and texts in the philosophy of language. More precisely, these examples are problematic not because they cannot, in principle, become part of our lives but because they are entirely severed from the domain of concern, in the Heideggerian sense, to which a living language belongs. Philosophy can quite easily lose touch with the actuality of speech. The above examples show how that happens when philosophy fails to acknowledge the ways a living language breathes, constantly invested in our human concern(s). Sentences such as "I met a man I'll call Binkley" may ring with wit, but they ultimately remain a dislocated parody of language. They remain detached from and indifferent to the concreteness of the human situation. More than anything else, they exemplify a philosophical deafness toward the ways language actually matters to us. This raises again the question of listening in philosophy. What does it mean to philosophically develop an ear for everyday language? This question is not asked in Anglo-American philosophy of language. Nor is it typically opened, albeit for the opposite reasons, by Continental philosophers, neither by Heidegger who dedicates himself to the complexity of singular poetic junctions, such as in Hölderlin, nor by Derrida for whom writing and difference are at the heart of meaningfulness.

The personal cannot be thought unless we turn—or return—to language in a manner that remembers the conversations, exchanges, words, and voices that matter—that have mattered—to us. And here our attunement to how language matters—to the affect of language—will find expression in the kind of examples we choose for speaking, philosophically, about language. It is, in other words, important for philosophy, and especially for a philosophy concerned with language, to acknowledge that the examples it chooses are not only rhetorical means of exemplification but are pieces of a reflected world—the soil from which reflection grows— whose relation with philosophical reasoning is complex and reciprocal and, as such, cannot be forced into a simple instrumental hierarchy. The examples we adopt should not be understood as merely corroborative illustrations or, conversely, as means of refuting certain given theoretical positions. If we wish to engage the language we speak, our examples must be part of a landscape that philosophy can neither possess nor generate from within itself, but can only explore, remember, illuminate, open up, reveal, and exist through, much as a painter—think of Cézanne—stands in relation to nature. Again, this is something that may be very difficult to do, but it may also be simple. Simple? We can never completely escape the fate of bad faith.

1. It's Funny

Yesterday, completely by chance, we met on the street. It had been a long time since we last saw one another. We stood face to face at the corner of a flower shop and a crowded café and did not know where or how exactly to pick up the conversation. We were clearly excited, but also restrained. I said something and then you said something. Exchanging roles, you said something and then I said something, and then there must have been a silence and, again, another exchange of the same sort. A conversation, in any case, did not transpire between the two of us. Nor did it seem that a real conversation could evolve at all. Eventually you said, "It's funny," or maybe what you said was, "It's kind of funny," or perhaps "It's really funny." But whatever it was that you actually said, it suddenly seemed very true to me. I could see how all this really was funny, and I said, "Yes, it's very funny," or something like that.

Yesterday, then, you said two or three words that today, in a different context, have become a "sentence": a simple sentence, ostensibly a declarative sentence, a sentence that spoke to me and that I clearly understood yesterday but whose meaning and understanding have become an issue to stumble over today. And so, even though our conversation did eventually take a more definite turn, I think that these words you said, if we go back to them, can open a path for us to further articulate the personal. But, first, we must be more clear about how the sentence you uttered evades standard philosophical categorization, about how an important dimension of your utterance is unavoidably obliterated by the very act of philosophical reconstruction.[2]

How would philosophy typically approach your saying that "it's funny"? There are, roughly, two distinct philosophical starting points for thematizing what you said, two different though not exclusive forms of localizing the meaningfulness of your speech.

First, the meaning of your utterance may be sought in the kind of relation language has to the world that allows our speech to say something about—to represent or depict—the suchness of things. That is, the meaningfulness of "it's funny" may be grounded in the representability of the factual order. On the other hand, the key to the meaning of your utterance may be approached in terms of the roles played by language in human interaction, in terms of language's anchorage within the domain of intersubjectivity, i.e., language's purposiveness and functionality, its drives and effects.

(A) Treating your utterance as a saying about the suchness of things paradigmatically implies that it be framed as an assertion or a statement whose inner form, to use Wittgenstein, is "this is how things are."[3] As such, your utterance is likely to fall into one of two more specific categories, either that of an objective or a subjective statement.

(A1) If your utterance is an objective statement, then it is, in principle, analogous to singular statements such as "it's gold" or "this metal is made of gold." Thematized as a statement of this kind, "it's funny" would seem to require an analysis of that which it states, that is, of its propositional content or the objective suchness of things—the facts—that it depicts. In these terms the meaningfulness of your utterance would seem to lend itself to an understanding based on its ability to accurately (or inaccurately) represent the facts of the matter. Just as the statement "it's gold" acquires its meaning through its relation with the fact that this metal is either gold or not, so does your saying "it's funny" become understood as relating to the world in a manner that is necessarily either true or false. Again, it is either true or false precisely because the suchness of the world to which it relates is simply what it is, just like the case with the given piece of metal before us that is either gold or not and that, if gold, renders the sentence "it's gold" true and, if not, false. Furthermore, this interpretation not only ties the meaning of your sentence to its truth conditions, but it locates this meaning within a wider relational space in which knowing a sentence's truth conditions always implies knowing many other things. These other things are not only the criteria for a sentence's correctness but also constitute different kinds of procedures for the sentence's assessment and verification, diverse options for its explication and justification, as well as a full load of inferences and implications ("given the number of gold bullion pieces before you . . . you can now tell . . . ").

(A2) Yet, given that your speech is informational in kind, it may also be argued that objectivity is not what your utterance is about, that your saying belongs, rather, to the no less common domain of subjective statements. As such, what you said—"it's funny"—is likely to be thematized on a par with such utterances as "it amuses me," "it tickles me," "it makes me laugh" or, alternatively, "it hurts me" and "it saddens or depresses me." Your utterance, in other words, may easily be understood to be a presentation of your own subjective experience or to be saying something only about the way the world appears to you. As such, it would have no general validity, carrying no implications or commitments as to the objective character of things themselves. When M says, for example, that he can't bear (going through) a certain medical treatment, this does not mean that this treatment is unbearable in any general sense.

Subjective statements are distinct from objective assertions in numerous respects. But despite the unique aspects of their "grammar" of use,[4] these statements are paradigmatically perceived as relying on and sharing the same fundamental meaning structure as objective statements. While subjective statements are statements about one's subjective domain of experience, they remain dependent on the same stringent truth conditions that determine the meaning of fact-depicting language. And so, while such sentences as "I'm tickled now" or "I'm aching now" do not seem to allow us to substantiate the facts of the matter in any objective manner, they still cannot be understood independently of the facts they purport to depict, facts that—to use Russell—"are what they are" and, precisely in being what they are, render these sentences necessarily either true or false. To put this generally, we may say that when an utterance such as yours is taken to be saying "something about something," the meaningfulness of your speech is paradigmatically understood on the basis of the propositional core of what you said, regardless of its objective or subjective perspective.

(B) However, as suggested, this is not the only prism through which the philosophical tradition tends to understand utterances such as yours. In particular, there are two well-established nonpropositional perspectives that are relevant to this discussion, two alternative ways for understanding what you said that remove your utterance from the hinges of its truth values. The first of these alternatives understands your sentence as expressive in essence. The second prioritizes the pragmatic aspects of your statement so as to identify its meaning with its performativity.

(B1) Expressivity: Thinking of your utterance as expressive in its essence shifts the interpretative focus from the descriptive or propositional aspects of the utterance to certain attitudes or emotions that characterize you as a speaker. To view your utterance in this way is to see that the words *it's funny* give spontaneous expression to a particular emotional state, mood, or feeling and do not depict or purport to depict any specific factual situation. Saying "it's funny" may be interpreted, in other words, as the kind of thing one says in one and the same breath with a smile or with laughter itself—just as the cry "it hurts!" is often a reaction to pain rather than a description of pain. This implies that there is no place for attributing truth or falsehood to your words. Your words only appear to be descriptive in character, but, in actuality, they are used in ways analogous to cries of joy, sighs of relief, murmurs of confusion—"wow," "this is just unbelievable" or "at last," "hurray," "enough!"

(B2) Performativity: Another, even more popular, nonpropositional way of reconstructing your speech is to thematize its meaningfulness in terms of its intrinsic embeddedness in the domain of linguistic action. According to this view, in saying "it's funny," you were, before anything else, doing something. Thus, bracketing the traditional sense and reference of your utterance, the key to understanding your speech act may be said to be found in the intended effects of your utterance. For example, your saying "it's funny" may be understood as a way of gracefully imposing closure on our conversation without explicitly ending it—that is, just like the kind of things we may say on the phone in suggesting that we want to hang up: "well, very good," "OK, then," etc. Or alternatively, your saying that "it's funny" might be understood as a mean for warming up the conversation, for breaking the ice, for releasing the conversation of its heaviness, a mean for escaping the dead end at which it seemed to have arrived.

How, then, are we to understand your utterance? Which of the aforementioned prisms can provide the interpretive key for unpacking your speech? Or better, why are none of the above options sufficient for truly engaging with what you said? To explain why this is so, it is necessary to recognize—and this is my starting point—that your speech addressed the very situation of which we were both part. In saying to me "it's funny," you actually spoke of our situation, of our being-in-the-world, and it was this world, or an aspect of it, that manifested itself in your words. You said something I understood, which was, for me, not trivial (that allowed me, for example, to see things in a new way) and with which I happened to agree, although I could have, in principle, also disagreed. In making a place for the concern of your words with the actuality of things between us, we see that the pragmatic and expressive options are insufficient. Even if we want to acknowledge certain pragmatic or expressive aspects of your utterance, we also need to see that these aspects are, in themselves, too narrow to develop a sense of the way in which your speech addresses the meaningfulness of our world.

This appears to be leading us back to option (A), the option for framing your utterance as a statement that, being either objective or subjective, calls for understanding it in terms of content. What kind of statement were you then making in saying "it's funny," an objective or subjective one? Was your utterance addressing the way things objectively are, depicting the fact that something is funny? Or did it purport only to describe your own subjective experience, the fact that for you things appeared to be funny? [5]

If we treat your saying as an objective statement depicting the objective state of things, it would be hard not to find ourselves compelled to agree that what you said is true only if certain conditions are met, only if the world is such that these specific conditions were part of it at the time of your utterance. More specifically, if when you said "it's funny" these truth conditions did not materialize in full, then your statement is false. This means that in saying "it's funny" you either lied (to me?) or you were simply wrong. But why does this analysis sound so awkward, if not ridiculous? Its irrelevance, or incompatibility, or perhaps (philosophical) violation is striking and indeed resonates. That is, the above analysis sounds unnatural because it unnaturally appropriates the particular event of speech that occurred between us. In order to recognize such a violation of language by philosophy, however, it is not enough to understand why the above analysis is wrong. There is no choice here but to develop an ear for it. To be more precise, an ear for language is a necessary condition for thinking about language philosophically. Can you hope to understand music, let alone be a musician, without an ear for it?

Let us be a bit more specific and point to certain features of your utterance that an objective analysis may not easily come to terms with. For example, if your utterance is an objective statement, how do we begin to specify what it is about? You said "it's funny," but what exactly does "it" refer to? Do we really want to understand you to be implying that there is some thing (in the world) that is the reference of the word *it*? And that that thing is funny? And what is that reference of the word *it*? What is the *it* that is said to be funny? Is it, for example, the *fact that* we are still—regardless of the time that has passed—unable to talk to each other? Or is the funny "it" the *fact that* maturing and gaining experience does not help us whatsoever? Perhaps it is the *fact that* we have not changed that is funny? And maybe you were altogether speaking of something else, perhaps the very coincidence—funny—of running into each other or, again, about the *fact*—how funny it is—*that* you can't walk in Tel Aviv without running into people you know? The point here is not how to identify the exact reference of your utterance. We need to ask, instead, whether we should seek at all to isolate a specific element in the situation and burden it with the task of being the reference of the word *it* in "it's funny." This seems to me to be a artificial (superficial?) way of handling that of which you spoke. Your words, as I heard and understood them, spoke about the situation in which we found ourselves, a situation that had many faces and folds of meaning, which enveloped us—an intricate net of varying senses that belie fine distinctions and whose multivarious constitution had no clear boundaries that could, as such, be referred to in any determinate manner.

There are further difficulties that arise from an objective analysis of your utterance. In particular, there is the need to flesh out an objective set of criteria for determining what is funny. The difficulty of such a task, together with the general indeterminacy of the "situation," may make a subjective analysis of your utterance a more popular option. That is, philosophy is likely to understand your saying "it's funny" as being concerned with your state of mind and, in particular, with the fact that you were amused or that you were suddenly feeling particularly whimsical or something of that sort. As such, your words would not be understood to have any real claim over the way things actually are between us. Their suggestiveness would not be regarded as a real indication of the fact that there is something funny in the situation itself but only that the situation is perceived or experienced by you as funny.

But, if you were so amused by things, why didn't you just laugh? Why didn't your face actually exhibit any trace of amusement, of that whimsical feeling? In other words, can we really settle for an interpretation that considers your sentence to be a representation of your mental state (one that again makes your words necessarily either true or false and you, naturally, either a speaker of truth or a teller of lies)? I think not. The reason for not doing so becomes apparent once we recognize that when you said "it's funny" you were not describing what you were experiencing but were, rather, saying something about the nature—"funny"—of our encounter, of the situation, the world, or the place in which we happened to be. Is this something that can be clearly proved or demonstrated? Probably not. But this does not mean that we cannot see, cannot develop a sensibility that would allow us to sense how superficial the subjective analysis is. And isn't such a sensibility already a part of our everyday life? It is present in the ways we go about language, even if we do not always explicitly come to terms with it. As such, it should not be forsaken when (we turn to) doing philosophy. We should not forget that to listen to the actuality of your words is to respond to *you*. In responding to you on that particular occasion, it was perfectly clear—though not in any reflective sense—that your words ("it's funny") did not confine themselves to, and in fact transcended, your subjective shell. They were in dialogue with that very encounter, open to what "has happened," to that which happened *there*, between two people who coincidentally met again (on the street).

Hence in order to understand your speech we need to make room for—to remain in touch with, or allow ourselves to be guided by—a pair of critical intuitions that at first might seem to be contradictory. On the one hand, it is important to see that what your speech opens up to is the actual texture of the things between us (and not any subjective perspective of them). On the other hand, we must also understand that the meaning of the world we share is never fully contained in objective self-sufficiency but, rather, unfolds in ways that are always essentially perspectival. The question is how to hold on to both these intuitions: how to accommodate the presence of a genuine tension between the ostensibly public and intimately private dimensions of our language.

We clearly cannot do so as long as we accept the form of propositions—or the structure of information—as our standard for encountering the meaningfulnes of things. Unless we release our thinking about language from the grip of the propositional, we shall remain blind—and deaf—to how language can speak about the suchness of the world without having to lose itself in the anonymity of the facts it depicts, how language succeeds in expressing the particularity of the self without becoming hermetic.

2. Aesthetic Judgment

One of the places I find most helpful in seeking to come to terms with your speech—in attempting to articulate a philosophical space in which your words could reverberate like they did yesterday—is Kant's understanding of aesthetic judgment. More specifically, I refer to the judgments concerning the beautiful or, as Kant calls it, the "taste of reflection" as opposed to the "taste of sense." For Kant, judging taste necessitates deep consideration since it entails an exceptional, perhaps even disconcerting, ambivalence that cannot simply be integrated into the transcendental framework within which he attempts to explicate the general power of judgment. The "puzzle,"[6] as Kant calls it, regarding the judgment of taste is this: while couched in subjective feeling, it nevertheless seems to have a "universal validity." The judgment of taste speaks, according to Kant, in a "universal voice" (59). Rooted as it is in subjectivity, aesthetic judgment cannot be reduced to (the privacy of) the subjective, because it reflects the actuality of things, doing so in a manner that "lay[s] claim to the agreement of everyone." Hence, according to Kant,

> This special characteristic of an aesthetic judgment [of reflection], the universality to be found in judgments of taste, is a remarkable feature not indeed for the logician but certainly for the transcendental philosopher. This universality requires a major effort on his part if he is to discover its origin, but it compensates him for this by revealing to him a property of our cognitive power which without this analysis would have remained unknown. *(57)*

This can be put another way: despite its legitimate claim for universality, aesthetic judgment does not evolve from and cannot be grounded in our objective knowledge about the world because it is not rooted in concepts but in a feeling. This means that it cannot simply be integrated into the general paradigm of (determinative) judgment Kant developed in the *Critique of Pure Reason*. The judgment of taste must itself be reckoned with because it resists explanation in the general terms of cognitive or logical judgments, i.e., the structure by which a particular is subsumed under a given rule or universal. And so, though Kant understands that unless he could bring the judgment of taste under unifying principles it would threaten the cohesiveness of his project, he remains committed to elaborating the intuition (or the discovery) that the form of our encounter with the beautiful is truly unique, that with beauty we open up to meaning (to the meaningfulness of the world) in a manner that is out of the ordinary in terms of our common patterns of engaging the intelligible. Our human responsiveness to beauty is unique, according to Kant, because it constitutes a form of human relationship to the world that precedes the opposition between subjectivity and objectivity. On the one hand, in judging something to be beautiful we find ourselves relating to a specific sensual manifold that, framed by the here and now, allows us to assume, expect, and even to require that the beauty that appears to us exists, beyond the privacy of our experience, in a manner that belongs to our shared situatedness. Very much as in the case of ordinary perception of things, the beauty of a rose, of a face, a lit street in the rain, appears to us as that which is "there" and is, as such, appreciated by anyone who shares our situation. At the same time, however, the appearance of beauty does not seem to have, at least not on the face of it, the kind of structure required for universal communicability, that is, a determinate structure of cognition. In aesthetic judgment our relation to the object allows its beauty to appear even though that object is not subjected to any given concept of understanding. We thus "speak of beauty as if it were a property of things" (56), but, since beauty appears to us independently of a determinate concept, our aesthetic judgment says practically nothing about the character or the properties of the actual object. It adds nothing to our cognition of the way things are. That is, despite the shared, public character of beauty's appearance, beauty remains external to the objective gear of the world. And despite the universal appeal of the judgment of taste, that judgment can never become integral to any objective discursive framework. Walking on the beach, for example, you pick up a shell. You say, "Look at how beautiful this is." Yet, unlike a statement such as "this is made of plastic" or "this is a dime," what you said about the beauty of the shell can neither be proven nor used in inferring additional information about the nature of the object (why would you want to do that anyway?). Again, we should remember, that although the judgment of taste cannot belong to the realm of judgments that are necessarily true or false, and cannot be part of the spectrum of judgments that are subjected to procedures of proof or refutation, its validity is nevertheless not restricted to—indeed, it immanently transcends—the space of private subjectivity. When you say, for example, that the road is beautiful, your judgment rests on a subjective feeling. At the same time, it necessarily, as Kant insists, breathes generality. When you say that the road is beautiful, the view you are expressing is clearly perspectival, since you are voicing your own feeling in regard to what *you* see, i.e., your own perspective on how the road appears to *you* as opposed, for instance, to the way it may appear to me. Still, we need to notice that the perspectival structure of your encounter with the beauty of the road is not something that belongs to your experience (is this what Husserl also means when he says that "experience has no perspective"?). This is because perspectival appearance is not the foundation but rather the affirmation of the shared character—the universality—of a public sphere in which, and only in which, the beautiful agrees to show itself. In saying that the road is beautiful, you are, in other words, speaking without the ability to establish the general validity of your words. This does not imply, however, that your words report a private event. On the contrary, if we focus on your private experience instead of recognizing how you speak of a view shared by the rest of us who are walking or riding along the road with you, then we would totally misunderstand what you said.

For Kant, as suggested, the unique judgment of taste is only the trigger for an investigation. He makes clear from the very beginning of the *Critique of Judgment* that the particularity of this judgment cannot be excluded from the general architectonic of his work, but must be brought "back home." For Kant, this integration assumes a typically transcendental move that I am not able and do not wish to pursue here. Let us turn back from Kant to the phenomenology of language, even if this means parting ways before glimpsing either the cellar foundations or the dramatic, often dizzying, high towers of the Kantian cathedral from which one might achieve a more perspicuous view—of the free play between the imagination and understanding—of what exactly happens there that allows us, as humans, to open up to beauty.

3. The Language of Taste

In returning to the phenomenon of language—which is itself less, and perhaps not at all, important to Kant—we observe that the uniqueness of the judgment of taste is twofold. Judging something to be beautiful is not only unique because it cannot be mapped out or charted within a framework governed by the objective-subjective dichotomy. It is also unique because its form of appearance typically conceals its very uniqueness. Conceals? How? When? Precisely when it appears: when it gets expressed in language. That is to say, when a judgment of taste is uttered, it has no identifying characteristics. It can pass right by you, perhaps even pass right through you, without exposing its identity. It exists incognito. This is because the judgment of taste so closely resembles—so easily assimilates with—that which it is not: a cognitive judgment. Kant was well aware of this silent, even misleading, linguistic presence of the aesthetic. Although he never explicitly takes issue with the significance of this similitude—probably because the phenomenon of language always remains of secondary importance to him—Kant is nevertheless so fascinated with this resemblance that he effectively makes it one of the leitmotifs of his discussion. Hence, for example, we "talk about the beautiful *as if* beauty were a characteristic of the object and the judgment were logical. . . . We talk in this way because the judgment does resemble a logical judgment" (54) and one "speaks of beauty [again] *as if* it were a property of things" (56). We may thus say that the form in which the judgment of taste appears is the form of "as if" or of similitude. This means that aesthetic judgment assumes a form of appearance that is likely to escape the attention of those who have not already made its acquaintance. This is because it bears no clear, distinct signs of—no a priori criteria for its—individuation. Identification of this form assumed by aesthetic judgment requires us to have both prior experience and a finely developed ear. It requires us to have what, in other contexts, would be understood to be the conditions of such enlightening encounters as "Wait . . . no . . . this must be . . . " or "What? I was sure that I was hearing . . . (Bach?)." In yet a different context, it is the kind of perceptiveness at play when we sense a touch of sadness in a cheerful face or hear the sound of longing in an otherwise sarcastic remark.

The ease with which the judgment of taste blends in with the general form of propositions is significant because it exemplifies, once more, how easy it is for assertive language (or propositional form) to dominate the grounds of the intelligible. In this respect, we may want to interpret Kant's attention to the particularity of the aesthetic as a gesture of resistance against the uniformity of the propositional. In particular, we may understand Kant's gesture toward the aesthetic as foreshadowing—as being a structural anticipation of—the kind of move Austin makes when he uncovers the unique presence of performative utterances at the very heart of constative language.[7]

The judgment of taste is like the performative, a form of meaningfulness that can only show itself if we resist the temptation of a propositional (that is, unifying and global) view of language. Unless we resist it, aesthetic language would, as Kant knew, remain indistinguishable from fact-stating language and would continue to pass as propositional, "oddly enough"—to use Austin again—"when it assumes its most explicit form."[8] For Kant, as suggested, the judgment of taste becomes an issue as part of a general attempt to explicate the power of judgment, that "mediating link between understanding and reason" (5). For our purposes, however, the ultimate goals of his agenda are less significant than is the intuition that informs Kant's project to begin with. This intuition—which Kant could not logically substantiate and yet to which he largely, even surprisingly, remains committed—is that the determinative structure of judgment cannot serve as the ultimate standard for the appearance of the intelligible and that, more particularly, our aesthetic engagement with the world defies that standard. But the implications of embracing the uniqueness of the aesthetic are more radical than the possibility of a local resistance to the propositional. If we think about Kant together with Austin again and recall how the latter's discovery of performatives leads to a complete reevaluation of the phenomenon of language, then we can, analogously, understand that in embracing the particularity of aesthetic judgment we have not only made room for a nonpropositional island of meaning but also have, in fact, taken the first steps in recovering for language the roots it has in such dimensions of experience as the aesthetic. That is, we have opened language to its own potential in a manner that ultimately subverts the hegemony of the propositional.

How can Kant illuminate, then, the words you said when we met yesterday, by chance, at the corner of that flower shop and crowded café?

4. The Phenomenality of Your Words (Language as a Phenomenon)

Kant couches the appearance of the beautiful in a particular kind of encounter with the world. This encounter, in which both the subject's interests and the object's telos are in repose, frees the sensual object from a determinative propositional structure. It allows the meaningfulness of a concrete "it" to appear unframed and makes room for this appearance (of beauty) in a manner that belongs neither to the viewing subject nor to the independent structure of the object. The form of such an encounter provides the only kind of soil in which, according to Kant, the beauty of the rose can grow and show itself to us. But the possibility marked by such an encounter, the possibility of a relationship with the world that allows meaning to appear in between the self-sufficient neutrality of objects and the partiality of subjective experience, is not exclusive to the experience of beauty. If we properly examine the question, we shall see that this possibility is conspicuously present in all regions of experience.

In this respect, the Kantian analysis of beauty ultimately tells us something important, not only about the character of aesthetic experience but about who we are as well—about the possibilities that are ours as humans. Just as Plato's treatment of beauty in the *Symposium*, for example, illuminates the erotic essence of our being and the absence that constitutes our existence as mortals, so Kant's aesthetic judgment reflects the structure of a human possibility that is integral to our being. That possibility is the recovery of the junction between or the mutual envelopment of subject and world that underlies the customary positioning of the I vis-à-vis the world. It is the possibility of encountering the meaningfulness of the world—we may even say of being-in-the-world—in a manner that is more original than and reaches underneath the clusters of sense and customary meaning formations born of our bipolar (subjective/objective) relation to the world. Was not this the kind of possibility Husserl envisions when he calls upon philosophy to return "to the things themselves"?

I think that a phenomenological interpretation of the inner form of the aesthetic is not only natural but is most needed here. Isn't beauty *the* phenomenon par excellence, the quintessence of phenomenality? Moreover, the model of beauty is phenomenologically helpful because it opens up the possibility of responding to levels of experience that the subject/object dichotomy as well as the thetic and teleological structures of meaning do not allow us to see, that is, the possibility of letting, as Heidegger puts it (when he interprets Husserl's dictum in the beginning of *Being and Time*), "that which shows itself be seen from itself" (58). In particular, the model of beauty allows us to free your speech—what you said yesterday—from the paradigmatic constraints of the propositional and to return to its actual unfolding as a meaningful utterance.

You said "it's funny." In saying that, your speech opened up to and reflected something of our situation, of our world. At the same time, however, it was concerned neither with an indifferent world of self-sufficient facts nor with the affected state of your subjectivity. Instead, your speech encountered meaning in a manner that reflects the form of your encounter with the world. The form of your situatedness—your being-in-the-world—was the inner form of your utterance. The character of your orientation in the world was such that it left that primary junction between you and world conspicuous enough for your speech to reflect it. Hence, in opening up to meaning, your speech was responding to a situation that was free to show itself (as funny) because of your particular orientation within that situation. Someone else, a person dominated by assertive, informational, or strictly instrumental norms, would have difficulty seeing that the situation was funny at all. For that person, the funniness of the situation cannot display itself, similar to the case of those who are blind to beauty (often intelligent persons look right through the beauty of things as if it were not there. Why are certain ways of life unable to make room for beauty?).

Your speech addressed our situation, and that situation showed itself in your speech. But this does not mean that your words had a distinct objective reference or that the so-called situation could possibly serve as such a reference. On the contrary, because of your location in, your being-in, that which showed itself to you, the situation of which you spoke did not take the form of a thetic presentation. It showed itself to you, rather, while remaining unframed. We cannot, consequently, hope to understand what your speech is about unless we make room for what Husserl, for example, characterizes as that "dimly apprehended depth or fringe of indeterminate reality."[9] Another way to put this is to say that the indeterminate horizons reflected in your speech are the horizons of our story, a story whose openness (to the future) cannot in principle be framed. We—you and I, our bodies, the window, the rose, time lost, time suspended, sense of humor, hopes, secrets, things left unsaid, things misunderstood, things deeply understood, our house, the kitchen, the laughs, the streets, the sea, poetry, and then, of course, that chance meeting yesterday, was it really such a coincidence?—are the (actual) horizons of that *it* of which you spoke when saying "it's funny."

Furthermore, despite its indeterminacy, the situation of which you spoke was not in any way less meaningful than a propositionally framed statement you could have possibly made about, say, politics, the weather, or about the fact that the café next to us has recently been renovated. That is, what you said was naturally interwoven into a discursive space—one whose history is ours—to which, as in the case of aesthetic judgment, the question of validity is not foreign. Your utterance was not a lonely shot in the dark but part of a dialogic matrix that allowed me to agree or disagree, to accept or argue against ("No, I don't think it's funny . . . it's just awkward" or "It's actually sad that . . . "), to be convinced or to try to convince you, to keep talking to you. In this sense, we may want to follow Kant and hear in your words that "universal voice" (of the aesthetic) that testifies to the manner in which your utterance transcends the privacy of the subjective and claims general validity for itself. But we also need to add a qualification. Although your utterance reflected the actuality of things, and did so by an appeal to a world that is always already intersubjective, it did not so much "lay claim to the agreement of everyone" as much as it addressed itself to me. You spoke to me.

This brings us to yet another and perhaps even more important sense in which our intersecting individuality—yours and mine—is crucial to (understanding) the meaningfulness of your utterance. I am thinking of the particular directionality of your speech: of the significance of the fact that *your* words were said to *me*, that *I* was the person to whom *you* said "it's funny." This is a fact that tends to be taken for granted if not completely trivialized by the paradigmatic addresser-addressee structure underlying theories of communication across the board.

What we thus need to recognize is that by conceptualizing our involvement in the speech situation in terms of the general and anonymous functionality of "communication poles" we are inevitably obliterating the original appearance (phenomenality) of your utterance. The meaningfulness of your speech would be lost if we abstract/extract what you said from its embeddedness in the singularity of *your* saying and *my* listening. That is to say, the meaning of your speech is so dependent on you being the individual you are—and on my singularity as the person you spoke to—that it cannot retain its significance when abstracted from our presence as singular individuals, when transposed onto a global space of logical possibilities. To be clear on the effects of such a transposition, consider, for example, how your words would resonate—what would happen to your speech—when presented from an "objective" point of view: "She told him that it was funny."

Hence, whereas strictly informational utterances such as the one made to you by the bank teller yesterday—"The transfer into your account was made. Your account now stands at $25"—naturally lend themselves to reiteration in objectified forms ("The bank teller said to him that the transfer to his account had been made and that now . . .), the case of your speech is different. Can you hear the difference? Can you hear how your saying changes when passed on or reproduced without special attendance to the roots it has in the concreteness of the lived situation and in the individuals involved?

Your saying "it's funny" belongs to the singular encounter between us, an encounter it would be wrong to understand only as a formal condition of your speech. This encounter is not simply the context or the specific background required for the informational or practical specificity of your words. It is not a neutral field of meaning in which we anonymously exchange pieces of ready-made language. Your speech was not part of a neutral exchange between an unspecified pair of addresser and addressee who, in this specific case, happened to be us. Rather, it grew out of a meeting whose essence was precisely the meeting between *you* and *I*. It was born of the singular encounter between us. In contrast to certain exchanges in which the individuality of the person to whom we're speaking may be less important to us—for instance, when we pay a toll on the highway—the kind of encounter we had yesterday was constituted of our unique, irreplaceable presence as the individuals we are. (Indeed, this meeting only became an issue precisely because I met you, and not just anyone else who happens to use words and phrases similar to yours.) You spoke to me and I was part of your words—your words took me in, I was in your language, your tongue—in the same sense that I was enveloped in your gaze, that it was my shoulder your fingers touched.

This is precisely where the personal begins to show itself, i.e., as the mark of our singular attachment to language, which finds its expression in the way language silently attaches, or even commits, itself to who we are. Hence the context of intimate conversations may make it somewhat easier to identify the presence of the personal, perhaps because, as friends, we naturally respect the idiosyncracies of each other's language. Take, for example, the case in which you say to a friend that you are simply unable to do what you want so much to do, what you know you can and should do. In saying that, you speak to her in a way she could not understand—as a friend she knows she could not understand—unless she manages to bracket and, at the same time, listen through the general (in this case contradictory) informational patterns exhibited in your speech. That is, unless *she* listens to *you* speaking to *her*, the *it* of which you are speaking—e.g., your inability—will remain covered up by the general senses of a neutral language, by a language that belongs to no one in particular and that can thus be utilized by anyone. I think that the conversations of friends—or, more generally, of persons close to, or intimate with, each other—is a good place to return to in order to recall that, contrary to what Heidegger contends, the public averageness of the "they" does not "proximally control every way in which the world and Dasein get interpreted." It is a good place to see for ourselves that what Heidegger calls "idle talk" is not all-encompassing. Hence, even if the reign of *das Man* poses a real threat to a genuine dwelling in our language, this does not mean that we should—on the contrary, if we wish to be open to the threat, then we clearly should not—accept the averageness of *das Man* as a structural condition of everyday intelligibility. We should not, in other words, internalize the totalizing affect of Heideggerian guilt. When we speak as friends, when I actually speak to you or you speak to me, our speech knows how to refuse the averageness of the "they." It resists being "glossed over as something that has long been well known." And this is actually what happened when we met on that street corner. In saying—to me— "it's funny," you were using words that are completely common and ordinary and yet what you said resonated, and resonated clearly, without being "passed off as something familiar and accessible to everyone."

The personal, however, is not only the mark of a language based on a preestablished intimacy. The personal exists between us as a present possibility, like a window waiting to be opened. This is a possibility that we may either embrace or ignore. Friends may speak to each other in ways that are forgetful of the personal, while strangers may speak in a personal voice.

Stopping at the light, we ask someone for directions. He says "take a left here and then another left at the second light." Under most circumstances what matters to us in this kind of encounter is getting the information we need. We relate to the speech of the other person only as a means of obtaining that information. In so doing, his individuality as a speaker does not concern us at all. We open up to his speech in a manner that renders his individual presence irrelevant. It seems to make no difference to us who the person is that is speaking to us. As far as we're concerned, he could be anyone else—anyone in his shoes; in fact, a speaking road map would do—provided that they can convey the relevant information. But, even if our interaction with the language of the speaker giving us directions is indifferent to his singular presence in that language, this does not mean that things cannot change on the spur of the moment.

The language of the other person may be full of surprises. To be open to language is precisely to accept language as a source of the unexpected. While providing the information we asked for, that speech of the other person may suddenly take a turn that cracks open the informational structure presupposed in this kind of conversation. This might be a slip of tongue, an awkward mispronunciation, a sudden silence, an outdated or a witty way of saying something, perhaps something altogether dazed in the presentation, or just something . . . a remark about . . . a certain word, the name of a place we haven't heard in years, a voice that . . . that reminds us of something else. The point is that we may suddenly find ourselves listening to a language that is no longer anonymous, even though we remain ignorant about the facts comprising the life of the person speaking to us. (An opposite kind of experience is one in which the language of a person known to us remains anonymous. When, while speaking to a neighbor or a colleague for almost an hour, you hear only reproductions of common patterns of speech—that may make much sense and be intelligent or even witty—you want to respond "knock knock, is anyone at home?").

The personal, in other words, may not be allowed to show itself. But this possibility is always there for us to embrace. And, even when it is supressed, it remains as, to use Husserl again, a "dimly apprehended depth or fringe of indeterminate reality." The personal continues to appear, to be present, in the form of that which has been ignored, just as the new kid on the block may shyly stand there for days, waiting to be acknowledged by the "gang." Aren't you the one who just moved into the orange house last month? You have a dog, right? When the moment of acknowledgment finally comes, its outward form is always so trivial. Nevertheless, this triviality does not diminish the preciousness of the moment. Viewed from a public, or propositional, perspective, the gesture of acknowledgment can say nothing new. It is structured as a language that simply folds the familiar onto itself, a language that only mirrors the obvious: "this is you" or "isn't this you?" But it is precisely in this fold that the familiar creates within itself, that a whole new world opens up.

CHAPTER 6
Personal Time

> *This conjoined itself with another, really, stupefying consciousness of a question that he would have allowed to shape itself had he dared. What did everything mean—what, that is, did she mean, she in her vain waiting and her probable death and the soundless admonition of it all—unless that, at this time of day, it was simply, it was overwhelmingly too late?*
> —Henry James, Beast in the Jungle

The personal lives in the tension that exists between a person's language and her individuality. We cannot encounter the personal unless we turn to language in a manner that acknowledges and actively embraces this tension. This can be done, however, only once we understand that the personal is not the dialectical counterpart of abstract content. Unlike propositional content, the personal is not abstract but always concrete, and yet its concreteness is not external to the appearance of meaning. On the contrary, the personal is the very fabric of meaning. It belongs to the phenomenon of language just as texture belongs to the visuality of a painting. In this sense, the possibility of recognizing the presence of the personal in language is somewhat similar to recognizing the presence of an actual brushstroke within the translucency of a Vermeer, for example. The revelation of a brush's motion, of a hand (that was once) at work, is a reminder. It reminds us that an abstract mind cannot paint and that the world can appear in paintings only through the singular intervention of a painter who, to use Merleau-Ponty, lends his body to the world.[1] Similarly, the language we speak can envelop the depths of a human world only through the personal conductivity, the idiosyncratic involvement, "the hand," "the fingerprint," of the individual who speaks. The personal is the physiognomy of language. It is the face that makes language human and that, as such, enables us to resist and oppose the fate of a world in which the rule of meaning is homogeneous and anonymous.

But, how does this human physiognomy show itself in language? Where exactly should we look for it? As suggested, the personal resides in the very things we say. But, this is not enough. In order to encounter the personal, we need to find a point of view in which the propositional no longer dominates our perception of ordinary language, a point of view in which content can reveal its indeterminate, nonpropositional depth. Nestled in the interstices of the intelligible, this depth never takes the form of a given fact (about language or meaning) and therefore cannot be read off language as one of language's positive facets. Furthermore, this depth continues to remain hidden when we attempt to transgress, turn our back on, or move to deconstruct the ordinary appearance of content in language.

We cannot see the latitude of the personal unless we actually turn to content. But, at the same time, we must not hurry to view content as the ultimate object of our perception of language. Instead, we need to look at content as a medium for stereoscopic vision, as a prism through which depth can show itself. We need to look right through the abstract field, the plane, the pane of pregiven logical possibilities that get framed in language and that philosophy so often privileges as the grounds of understanding. In encountering the personal, our gaze must learn how to wander through the uniformity of language's thetic structures and, guided by the actual horizon of concrete intelligibility, look after the vanishing point of speech.

1. Time Is Past

In this chapter I wish to continue the concrete elaboration of the personal by focusing, this time, on a written proclamation. The example I wish to discuss is a somewhat colloquial, nontheoretical remark that Wittgenstein makes at the end of the preface to his

Philosophical Investigations. Made at the edge of or, better, at the point of entering into philosophical discourse, Wittgenstein's remark is a good place for continuing the exercise of our philosophical ear. The preface to Wittgenstein's *Investigations* ends in the following way:

> I should have liked to produce a good book. This has not come about, but the time is past in which I could improve it.[2]

These lines echo a sentiment perhaps inherent in the predicament of philosophical writing as such. However, they first of all express Wittgenstein's personal struggles in writing the *Investigations*: with the problem of writing (in) philosophy, with the predicament of his own writing, and with the question of fulfillment in his life through writing. The general tone of these lines, their pessimism, their self-criticism, and their sense of defeat, together with a kind of self-possession and determination, are not untypical of Wittgenstein. They reflect his diary entries and, in an interesting play of mirrors, the lines he had written twenty-seven years earlier at the end of his preface to the *Tractatus*.[3]

Wittgenstein was not satisfied with the *Investigations*. As we know, he ultimately withdrew the manuscript prior to publication and never again tried to publish the work that was so important to him. But the closing lines of Wittgenstein's preface not only give voice to his dissatisfaction or regret. Nor are they an adoption of a rhetoric of apology. Wittgenstein is actually saying something quite specific: that, despite his desire and intent, he has failed to write a book that meets his expectations, that he is unable to improve the manuscript he has written, unable to turn it into the good book he had hoped for. There is something puzzling, even unsettling, here. If Wittgenstein is really unsatisfied, why does he not continue to work on his book, trying to make it better? What are the grounds for declaring—say, in January 1945, the date of the preface—that the writing of this "unfinished" book is completely finished? What unsettles us here is not so much Wittgenstein's failure to satisfy his initial expectations and write a "good book" but rather his unexplained and, at the same time, complete acceptance of the current condition of his manuscript as final, as done, as a fait accompli. How should we understand then the tension between the clear and definite manner in which Wittgenstein presents impossibility as part of his life and the complete absence of any factual grounds that could uphold the meaning of this expressed impossibility?

While leaving the facts of his situation unspecified, Wittgenstein nevertheless does tell us something important about the condition by which his writing has come to its end. Wittgenstein tells us that from the point of time—in time—in which he writes the preface time itself seems to have already exhausted itself. According to Wittgenstein, not only has the present outcome of his writing failed to meet his past—his initial—intentions and hopes but it has also failed to make a possible place for a future. That is, for Wittgenstein, a good book can no longer be written since it is too late for that—"the time is past."

What exactly is Wittgenstein saying when he speaks of time as that which, in having passed, does not allow him to become the writer of a better book? Wittgenstein makes it clear that the book he hoped for will not be written. It will not be written because the time in which it could have been written has passed and is past. But what is the status of this assertion? Is time really in the past? Is it no longer available for Wittgenstein's writing? In what sense does time rescind the possibility of realizing Wittgenstein's inspirations? In what sense does the passing of time separate Wittgenstein from his aspirations? How should we understand Wittgenstein's saying about time? And what would it mean to take his allusion to time seriously?

The complexity of Wittgenstein's remark is indicative of a particular tension that resonates in his words, a tension between the objective availability of time, i.e., the fact that Wittgenstein seems to have no impending time limitations, and the sense in which, for him, time is already over. This tension between the private and public meaning of time is crucial for understanding what Wittgenstein is saying. And it is precisely because of the irreducibility of this tension in Wittgenstein's language that I find his remark about time to be a fruitful case study for developing our thinking about the personal.

2. Time, Language, and Possibility

Wittgenstein speaks of a possibility that had once claimed his future, but one that, in the flow of time, has become empty. He wanted to "produce a good book. This has not come about, but the time is past in which [he] could improve it." The fact that an open possibility withers and falls into an abstract reservoir of biographical counterfactuals is an ordinary part of everyday parlance. And, in this respect, Wittgenstein's remark belongs to an idiomatic family of ordinary rhetorical and discursive forms to which we turn when speaking of those possibilities—once open to us—that have lost their potential or vitality. These are forms of saying that "this can no longer happen," or "there's no time left," or "we missed the moment or the time we had for" or that "now it is too late for that." It was, for example, so important for me to tell him how I feel about . . . but it is too late for that now, and the wheel cannot be turned back. Time is past and you can no longer, as you say, have a baby. It is too late, at this point in your life, to become a professional musician; too late, under the circumstances to save his spectacular career. It is too late for the Beatles, now with Lennon and Harrison gone, to have a reunion, etc.

These example are varied. And this is because there are more ways than one to speak of those possibilities that time has taken away from us. There are more ways than one to think of the relationship between the passing of time and the appearance of an impossibility. However, as we consider this discursive family, we see that it exhibits a few dominant patterns that philosophy is inclined to privilege. D. tells us, for example, that he missed out on a financial opportunity that would have completely changed his life and the lives of his children. Years ago he was offered a large piece of real estate for a ridiculously low price. The area, however, was considered a waste land and so he naturally took some time to think it over. When he finally decided to go through with the daring purchase, it proved to be too late. The land had already been sold. Today, as everyone knows, it has become one of the most trendy neighborhoods of the city.

Indeed, when we speak of possibilities no longer open to us, we often refer to time as a means—a frame of reference—for presenting the specific facts that constitute the impossibility that concerns us. Such a language of time typically serves as a way for framing the fact of impossibility. When we acknowledge that it's too late to catch the train we accept the impossibility of riding on that train today. We missed it. We understand that the facts of our situation—e.g., the distance between our specific location and the train station—allows no possibility to take it today. We could have reached the train on time if things had gone differently: if we had packed earlier, or had not met a long lost friend, or hadn't sat for coffee with him. If, after a fascinating, or perhaps just a nostalgic, conversation we suddenly take our leave, our friend would be right to tell us that it is now too late: there is simply no way one could make it in four minutes to the train station on the other side of the city. Our friend would be expressing the fact that the time frame available to us is not sufficient in order to catch the desired train. ("It takes at least ten to fifteen minutes to get there," he says, "and just look at the traffic.") He is pointing out the facts of our world, that whether we like it or not the train will leave without us.

When the detective on TV says "It's too late," he means that the girl is dead. The fact is, the girl is dead. From a slightly different perspective the fact is that, despite his great effort, the detective failed to save the girl's life. "Too late" is exclaimed after the fact. Had he arrived before the murderer to the art dealer's shop things would have turned out differently. But there was no way for him to know where to find the girl (at least not until he traced the phone call). He made no mistakes. And, as his chief assures him, he should definitely not feel guilty.

For the detective, or for one hurrying to her train, time manifests itself in a twofold manner. It is available as a commodity of sorts, one we need but only possess by consuming. That is, it can only be ours on condition that we use it up and so lose it: "Will there be enough time?" "There is no more time left." Time is also, however, the structure and the measure of availability of that commodity. In this context, the desired possibility is dependent on the availability of time, an availability to which we typically relate through its public, objective, and datable features. We want to know, for example, *how much* time is left. The only thing that matters to the detective is to make it to the art dealer's *before* the murderer gets there. Hence, in speaking of time's availability, or unavailability, we are mapping the fact of possibility or impossibility onto the axis of publicly measured time as constituted by the order of "before" and "after." To say that "it's too late" is, thus, a manner of holding together, or apart, of juxtaposing or of comparing—and this can be done with regret, longing, provocation, indifference, etc.—two sets of factual (essentially atemporal) states of affairs: the situation after a certain point in time, t, and the one before t. This is either a factual condition dominated by an impossibility or a factual condition characterized by its openness toward that possibility (catching the train, saving the girl). The focal point of such phrases is, in any case, not time or temporality but the impossibility integral to the after t facts. This can be seen with special distinctiveness in the relatively common cases when phrases such as "it's too late" completely lose their temporal nuance and simply indicate the fact that something is impossible. Too late, as said by the shop owner locking up, the waiter putting up the chairs in the restaurant, or the clerk who refuses to process your application forms.

However, in speaking of time and impossibility in this way, ordinary language often puts us in a position that all too readily allows us to level our temporal experience and forget the actual forms of our involvement with time. A language of facts is typically a language of repressed temporality. This is a language in which the temporal unfolding of a person's life can only become meaningful through the form of an objective linearity that is regulated by the relation of "before" and "after." In a fact-depicting language the actual passage of time is reified and the articulation of the individual's temporal experience is confined to an anonymous, average, and datable scale of measurement: the so-called axis of time. When temporality functions in language merely as the quantifiable form of the factual, the actuality of time is lost. In such a language, however, we not only remain strangers to the "invisible progress," to use Bergson, "of the past gnawing into the future,"[4] but, furthermore, we erase the essential uniqueness of our personal involvement in the unfolding of our time *as* a lifetime—the singular life that is yours, hers, or mine. By primarily relating to time as a homogenous sequence of "nows," our language encourages us to suppress the entangled character of our finite temporal existence. But in living toward our death or, better, in living our life, we do not relate to time by gradually filling in a vacant sequence of homogenously given "nows." And we never, at any single moment, occupy a neutral position in the flow of our time. Time is intrinsically directional, and this directionality is what we are. In other words, when our language objectifies time and the possibilities that time opens and closes for us, we are inclined to elide the sense in which an individual is singularly situated in the current of her time, in the time that she *is*.[5]

Furthermore, as seen in earlier chapters, this ordinary factual attitude is often perpetuated when philosophy embraces facts (or propositions) as its standard of intelligibility. Operating within the context of a propositional picture of language, philosophy characteristically offers two basic strategies for dealing with the meaning of such utterances as Wittgenstein's "time is past." These strategies issue from the common, almost built-in, philosophical tendency to determine, as a precondition for any encounter with the phenomenon of meaning, whether or not the utterance under consideration consists of a representation of facts: whether or not it can be said to have a genuine cognitive content and thus serve as a candidate for bearing truth (i.e., having a truth value). When an utterance is understood as a factual statement, its interpretation typically proceeds in terms of language's relation to the facts it depicts (its truth conditions). If understood as a nonfactual proclamation, the meaningfulness of language is typically tied to the utterance's emotive, expressive, or performative qualities and would accordingly be understood in terms of the mood or the emotional attitude it expresses or its intended effects.

This implies that Wittgenstein's remark must be either a factual statement or a nonfactual one. There is a fact of the matter here, and there's no way around it: If Wittgenstein's utterance is nonfactual, it might be said to illuminate for us some aspect of Wittgenstein's emotional attitude (e.g, an expression of regret, an apologetic gesture, a plea for . . .), but it cannot provide an understanding of the situation itself. If, on the other hand, Wittgenstein's saying is factual, then it is necessarily either true or false. If it is false, then the impossibility of which Wittgenstein speaks did not actually occur. But, if the claim is true, then it is indeed the case that Wittgenstein could not improve the book that left him unsatisfied. And this impossibility stems directly from the facts of the world. In other words, within a propositional picture of language the meaning of those possibilities and impossibilities that we face in life is necessarily reduced to the form of a factual constellation: the term *impossibility* can be genuinely applied to a situation only if its necessity can be read off from the facts by means of general reasoning. Accordingly, if one asks why it is too late, or impossible, for you to talk things over with your father, the answer is that he died a year ago. The fact that he is dead implies—through its location in the space of reasons—that you cannot meet him and that, of course, you cannot talk to him as you had hoped to do. The general reasoning is this: since it is impossible to converse with the dead, and it is a fact that your father is dead, then it is impossible for anyone to talk things over with your father, including yourself. This is precisely the logic of the propositional, the basis of which is the assertion of an identity between you, the singular individual, and anyone else occupying your position. It is impossible for you because it is impossible for anyone in your position.

Now, this is precisely where the singularity of Wittgenstein's saying, where the singularity of his being in language disappears. Once a fact-depicting language has taken over any alternative understanding of the relation between temporality and possibility, the general meaningfulness of neutral facts become the only basis for articulating the presence of the impossibility of which he speaks. In other words, by tending to the impossibility described by Wittgenstein solely in terms of the facticity of his situation—of the specific (psychological, physical, historical) facts constitutive of his condition—one robs Wittgenstein's speech of two crucial, interconnected dimensions. The propositional not only turns the very passage of time, Wittgenstein's singular entanglement in time, into an external, superfluous aspect of that impossibility, but it also effaces the personal—idiosyncratic—essence of this impossibility.

The personal perishes when we put it into the straightjacket of the propositional. The rustling of its temporality cannot be heard when we allow the propositional to govern our attachment to language. Indeed, the philosophical elision of the personal grows out of certain, often dominant, modalities of our everyday being in language. Yet, although on certain occasions ordinary language seems to level, hide, or distort the individual's singular entanglement with time and possibility, this is not a general predicament of everyday language. In other words, even if our deafness to the personal is a symptom of certain forms of captivity in ordinary language, it is nevertheless not a sign of any structural inability on our part. Our ears are good enough. They can hear the reverberation of time in language if only we allow them to do so.

To put this in the form of a question: is the common (fact-depicting) way of accounting for the death of a possibility really exhaustive of the ways we actually speak? I think not, and it is precisely in this context that Wittgenstein's invocation of time becomes so relevant. Wittgenstein speaks of the connection between time and impossibility in a voice whose uniqueness is important for us to understand. This uniqueness does not stem from the attempt to transgress the limits of the ordinary but springs, rather, from the very heart of ordinary expression. More specifically, while using familiar terms, Wittgenstein's allusion to time is grounded neither in a clear temporal sequence nor in any specific factual situation that can explain the impossibility of which he speaks. Wittgenstein adverts to the passing of time in a manner that leaves unclear what the particular facts of his situation are and why they constitute a dead-end for his writing. But, more important, what is unique in Wittgenstein's statement is not its lack of proper factual support—this could, in principle, be supplied with additional details—but that such factual support—a full picture of the facts—cannot in itself account for the impossibility at the heart of Wittgenstein's situation. Wittgenstein speaks of an actual impossibility. But the necessity of this impossibility cannot be read off the facts of the world. He speaks of an ordinary kind of impossibility that, in a propositional space of meaning, can only appear as a lacuna.

3. Time Prefaced

But the fact that the personal dimension of Wittgenstein's remark cannot be seen from a propositional point of view does not imply that this lacuna is meaningless. It only implies that we need to find a perspective in which the meaning of Wittgenstein's saying could resonate in a new way. In looking for such a perspective, it may be specifically helpful to recall that Wittgenstein's remark about time appears in a preface to a philosophical work. In philosophical writing the preface typically marks the very edge of the philosophical text. The preface is a text that typically springs from reflexivity, but, at the same time, it is usually not reflective in the same sense that philosophy is. This is due to a certain transformation the writer's persona undergoes in entering philosophical discourse, in pronouncing the first line, taking the first step, on philosophy's stage. The preface is a place of transition, a waiting room, a foyer, a hall of departures. In the preface the philosopher speaks in the voice of a person waiting for the train to leave, waiting to board an airplane. Time is suspended. The journey has not yet begun, but the philosopher has already left home. The preface appears as an "in between." It is this "in between" that must be traversed in order to get from the ordinary (or from everydayness, i.e., home) to the place from which one "sees the world rightly."[6]

To put this in a slightly different way, we may say that the preface is usually the one place in the philosophical text in which the memory of the ordinary is, by convention, kept most alive. The preface is an area of the philosophical text in which the philosopher's work conventionally appears within the horizons of the philosopher's autobiography. While the canonical text of philosophy respects the opposition between the universality of the philosophical voice and the singularity of the autobiographical voice, this common opposition does not seem to hold in the preface. The preface is the meeting place of the autobiographical and the philosophical. It is, on the one hand, the place for acknowledging the role that autobiography has in bringing the philosopher to the opening of his text. But it is also and perhaps more dominantly understood as the place in which the philosopher is expected to say good-bye, to turn his back on, leave behind the burden of his autobiography to ensure a proper entrance into philosophical discourse.

The preface thus marks a unique moment in the philosophical text. This is the last moment before the philosopher's voice changes. As its Latin etymology suggests, the preface is what is said beforehand (*prae* = pre, *fari* = to say). It is a presaying. The philosophical preface is a saying that comes before philosophy speaks. Yet this should not be understood only in terms of the fact that the preface appears before—that it leads into—the philosophical text. The preface precedes philosophy in the sense, rather, that it opens to meaning in a way that is prephilosophical. The preface is, in itself, a saying—a mode of speech—that comes before philosophy; it is a saying whose language is there before philosophy begins, a language that enables philosophy to leave home and be on its way, and yet it is also a language that, as we've seen, is easily forgotten once philosophy spreads its wings.

All this makes the language of the philosophical preface particularly relevant for our thinking about the place and presence of the personal in the neighborhood of philosophy. Focusing on the relation between a text's saying and its presaying enables us to focus, as we've done in earlier chapters, on the question of beginning in philosophy. Why is it important for philosophy to remain intimate with its own beginning? How can philosophy begin without misplacing the personal? What does it mean for philosophy to embrace its own presaying?

We have seen that the personal cannot grow in a language that internalizes the abstract and general forms of reflection as its standard. Indeed, since the language of the personal is one that refuses to become a part of the global order of the thinkable, the presence of the personal may be easier to detect by focusing on the kind of prefatory language we find in the preface. Yet, in focusing on the preface, it is important to notice that its prefatory language is not genuinely a language of beginning. That is to say, the notion of *beginning* is, in itself, insufficient for coming to terms with the temporal horizons of the appearance of the personal. To put this more directly, prefaces do not actually emerge at the beginning of a philosophical investigation but are characteristically written with the closing of a philosophical project. Prefaces typically presuppose a point of view from which the philosophical text appears as a complete whole, as an essentially finished work, and, in this respect, the complexity of a preface's temporal horizons cannot be reduced to a simple order of "before" and "after." The language of "beforehand" turns out to be a language of "afterward," since the preface allows the philosophical text to begin only after the text has found closure. Another way to put this is to say that the language of the preface has a peculiar temporal constitution. It unfolds as the language of a beforehand that originates from text's ending. And it is a language of an afterwards that unfolds as a beginning. The preface is neither a before nor an after but rather the merging of before and after—the before-after—of the philosophical text. In the preface horizons meet or, better, the preface is a part of the text in which the meeting of horizons is somewhat easier to notice.

Noticing this indissoluble temporal knot operative as the horizons of writing will prove important for our understanding of Wittgenstein's remark. In this context we may furthermore notice that in the history of philosophical prefaces, the topos of time is not only extremely prevalent but also serves as an idiom for the tangled relationship of the philosopher and his work. Let us then take another step in the direction of Wittgenstein's exclamation by situating his words within the context of four other very different philosophical prefaces or openings in which a philosopher thematizes his work in relation to the pending horizon of time. Consider, for example, the opening of Descartes's *Meditations* together with the preface to Kant's third *Critique*. And, then, the preface to Heidegger's seventh edition of *Being and Time* and Quine's preface to the second edition of *The Pursuit of Truth*.

(A) RENÉ DESCARTES, OPENING OF *MEDITATIONS* (1642):

I realized that it was necessary, once in the course of my life, to demolish everything completely and start again right from the foundations if I wanted to establish anything at all in the sciences that was stable and likely to last. But the task looked an enormous one, and I began to wait until I should reach a mature enough age to ensure that no subsequent time of life would be more suitable for tackling such inquiries. This led me to put the project off for so long that I would now be to blame if by pondering over it any further I wasted the time still left for carrying it out.[7]

(B) IMMANUEL KANT, PREFACE TO THE *CRITIQUE OF JUDGMENT* (1783):

With this then I conclude my entire critical enterprise. I shall proceed without delay to the doctrinal one, in order to snatch from my advancing years what time may yet be somewhat favorable to the task.[8]

(C) MARTIN HEIDEGGER, PREFACE TO THE SEVENTH EDITION OF *BEING AND TIME* (1953):

While the previous editions have borne the designation "First Half," this has now been deleted. After a quarter of a century, the second half could no longer be added unless the first were to be presented anew. Yet, the road it has taken remains even today a necessary one, if our Dasein is to be stirred by the question of Being.[9]

(D) W. V. O QUINE, PREFACE TO THE SECOND EDITION OF *THE PURSUIT OF TRUTH* (1992):

In May 1990, a mere four months after this book first appeared , I was in the gallant little Republic of San Marino for a week-long international colloquium on my philosophy. Six month later I was in medieval Gerona, in Catalonia, giving the Josep Ferrater Mora Lectures—fifteen hours of them and five of discussion. . . . The busy months of preparation and the stimulating exchanges on these occasions sparked thoughts that would have made for a better book if the chronology had been inverted. I am approximating such an inversion as best as I can by this early revised edition.[10]

A–B) "I shall proceed without delay . . . "

In the first two examples Descartes and Kant express a similar attitude toward time. Both attend to their philosophical project with a clear understanding that time is running out. Descartes speaks to us from the "now" of the first day of the *Meditations*, while Kant stands at the completion of the third *Critique*, looking ahead to new avenues he still wants to explore. Descartes presents his experimental project as occuring "once in the course of . . . [a] life," an occasion for which he had carefully organized "a clear stretch of free time," an event—precious, singular, and dramatic—for which he had seemingly long been waiting. For Kant, the drama of philosophy took the form of a long-term—a life-long—"enterprise" that now belongs to his past. Descartes insists on finally beginning (from the beginning). Kant searches for the proper ending. But, despite these significant differences, both Kant and Descartes write, or engage in philosophy, in the face of finitude, facing the precarious and limited availability of time. The horizon of time is still open, but neither can take for granted that it will continue to be open for long. For both of them time is what runs out, making no exceptions. It will run out on them too. Descartes knows that he cannot postpone his engagement with the *Meditations* any longer. If he "wasted the time still left," the significant moment for which he has waited might escape him forever. Kant, slightly less anxious perhaps, is determined to "proceed without delay" to his next project before it becomes too late.

This preoccupation with time is significantly different, however, from the way time becomes relevant to Wittgenstein. While Descartes and Kant think of time in terms of its decreasing availability, or its approaching end, for Wittgenstein the finitude of his allotted time is not, in itself, an issue. Wittgenstein speaks of an impossibility that is not directly tied to the fact that a person's life must ultimately come to an end. That is, he is not so much interested in the time frame still available to him as he is concerned with the actual passing of time within this time frame. Wittgenstein's remark is not concerned with the lack of time or with time's unavailability, but rather with the way time *is* available, with the presence of time or the experience of time—time that, being in the present, is nevertheless past.

C) "After a quarter of a century..."

The crux of Heidegger's preface is an announcement of a change, or a turning point, in his relation to the work he had written a quarter of a century before. The 1927 edition of *Being and Time* consisted of only a portion of Heidegger's intended project. Thus, it appeared for years as an unfinished text—a "First Half"—awaiting completion. For Heidegger, the book's seventh German edition was an opportunity to change the formal status of his work and grant it closure by deleting the mark of its incompleteness or openness. Heidegger explains that, "after a quarter of a century, the second half could no longer be added unless the first were to be presented anew." That is to say, once time was past, it was futile for him to pursue the initial objective of his project.

Heidegger evokes the passing of time in a manner similar to that of Wittgenstein. For both, "time is past." This very fact that it is past and belongs (in the particular way it does) to what has passed is present in their lives in a manner that keeps them from bringing the project for which they will (have) become most remembered to completion. Underlying this similarity is a fundamental difference, however. For Wittgenstein the passing of time connotes a personal failure. Heidegger is ultimately not affected by time. Whereas Wittgenstein finds himself captured by time, the weight of time constitutes no burden for Heidegger, whose personal preface is, like his philosophical work, entirely future oriented. When Heidegger acknowledges that the "second half [of the book] could no longer be added," he does not understand that impossibility as a surrender to the passing of time but, on the contrary, as a victory of the future over the past. In announcing his decision to delete from *Being and Time* the mark (the "First Half") of an unfulfilled promise, Heidegger is not seeking to come to terms with the incompleteness of his past (work) but only to emancipate the future from the persisting demands of the past. To put it differently, Heidegger is erasing the debt left open from his past—his debt to his past—by underplaying the fact that his past is condemned to remain unresolved (forever). Is Heidegger's attitude in line with his statement that the "authentic person always has time," or is this somehow analogous to the way Heidegger deleted in 1935 his dedication to Husserl, which initially opened *Being and Time*? Are those two options mutually exclusive?

D) "If the chronology had been inverted..."

In the preface to the second edition of *The Pursuit of Truth*, Quine speaks of his relation to time and possibility in a manner that, at a first glance, might seem similar to Wittgenstein. Quine is not concerned with temporal finitude but with the availability of time. In the months that passed after the publication of his book, Quine arrives at new "thoughts that would have made for a better book if the chronology had been inverted." From the perspective of a few months, or almost a year, Quine understands that his book is not as good as he thought at the time of publication. For Quine, however, in contrast to Wittgenstein, the fact that he produced a book at a certain point in time that no longer meets his present expectations is not in any way final (or fatal), or, in other words, it is final only in a trivial, matter-of-fact sense.

Quine acknowledges the fact that the book he produced in 1990 was not as good as it could be. But with the passage of time and the publication of a better book (that is, the revised edition), this fact loses all its weight and becomes a mere piece of information about the past. Whereas the irrevocable passage of time is described by Wittgenstein as a source of paralysis, Quine responds with special activity, suggesting a challenge—even if only a rhetorical one—to the irreversibility of time. Quine not only differs in temperament (optimistic? industrious?) from Wittgenstein, but he also clearly differs from him in the way he understands the connection between "philosophy" and "work" or in his understanding of the nature of and his expectations about the writing of philosophy. But, for our purposes, we shall only focus on the place of temporality in the statements of these two philosophers. For Quine, as suggested, the fact that time has passed is meaningful only as a form of information. Thus, when he glances back at the passage of time, the only thing Quine can see—the only thing that appears to him—is a measurable interval consisting of a series of discrete events.

These events are chronologically ordered. They occur one after the other, or one during the time of the other, leading to the ultimate occasion in the series, which is the writing of the book's new preface in the present. For Quine, in other words, the passing of time—of his time—is a "chronology." It is an order of discrete temporal points of reference. In a chronology the events of time are externally, even if causally, related to one another, and it is precisely this externality that allows Quine to quip about approximating the inversion of the chronological order.

Underlying Quine's remark we can thus find a picture of temporality (of his own being in time) that may serve well as an epitome of philosophy's consistent failure to hear the personal. Hence, although Quine does speak about actual events that occurred *in* time, for him time is more of an abstract coordinator, a semantic space that enables us to speak of events rather than something that itself occurs and whose occurrence, or presence, is fundamental to who we are. In Quine's language time can become meaningful only in the form of an abstract, public, and entirely homogeneous, scale, in which a sequence of uniformly vacant moments are always waiting—and always in the same manner—to be used up and filled in with contents: "in May 1990," "a mere four months after," "a week-long colloquium," "six month later," "fifteen hours [of lectures] and five of discussion," "busy months of preparation," "stimulating exchanges on these occasions." Would it be possible to understand what Wittgenstein says about time in this kind of temporal framework?

On this point, let us notice that Quine's personal attitude toward time matches his philosophical treatment of the language of time in his classic work *Word and Object*, which argues that in "understanding the referential work of language and clarifying our conceptual scheme"[11] a new regimentation of language is necessary. This would include, among other diversions from ordinary language, an "alignment of time with space," that is, a canonical notation for treating "time as space-like." For Quine, "tense then is to give way to such temporal qualifiers as 'now,' 'then,' 'before t,' 'at t,' 'after t,' and to these only as needed" (172). Hence, for example, "taking the present tense as timeless always, and dropping other tenses [is an] artifice [that] frees us to omit temporal information or, when we please, handle it like spatial information. 'I will not do it again' becomes 'I do not do it after now' where 'do' is taken tenselessly and the future force of 'will' is translated into a phrase 'after now,' comparable to 'west of here'" (170). More generally,

> Each specific time or epoch, of say an hour's duration, may be taken as an hour-thick slice of the four-dimensional material world, exhaustive spatially and perpendicular to the time axis. . . . We are to think of t as an epoch of any desired duration and any desired position along the time axis. Then, where x is a spatiotemporal object, we can construe "x at t" as naming the common part of x and t. Thus, "at" is taken as tantamount to the juxtapositive notation illustrated in the singular term "red wine." Red wine is red at wine. *(172)*

With this in mind we may better understand the motivation for Quine's remark about inverting his biographical chronology, a witticism that exemplifies how deep the difference is between his and Wittgenstein's attitudes. Whereas Quine's spatial language can represent "any desired duration and any desired position along the time axis," it completely obliterates any sign of duration itself, or of what Bergson calls *durée*. More particularly, by representing time in a manner that leaves no trace of the flowing character of time, Quine adopts a point of view from which time's directionality no longer seems very crucial. On the time axis all points and all epochs have the same (logical) status. They are all equally emptied of the unique presence that makes them distinctive and sets them apart as moments of the "now," i.e., moments that "are," moments of the past that are "no longer," and moments that are "not yet." That is to say, they are denied any difference—so crucial to the way we experience time—between the kinds of existence that the past, present, and future have in our lives. When mapped onto the time axis—a representation whose units are essentially atemporal—time unavoidably appears to Quine as only superficially connected to the fact that its movement is future bound, that the consummation of the present leaves a (trodden) past behind while opening up to a new future, rather than the other way around. Quine's remark about the inversion of time actually accentuates his logical perspective of time, a perspective that reduces his temporal existence to a homogeneous sequence of events and epochs, a sequence that remains unvaryingly the same even when inverted or looked at backward. It is clear that the thought of inverting one's biographical chronology can have no place in Wittgenstein's preface. This is not because of any reluctance on the part of Wittgenstein to challenge—or, like Quine, to play with—the idea of the reversibility of time. But it stems, rather, from Wittgenstein's unwillingness to understand his biography in terms of a chronology.

4. Perhaps Present

We are in a position to return now to Wittgenstein's remark.

> I should have liked to produce a good book. This has not come about, but the time is past in which I could improve it.

What then is Wittgenstein saying here? Wittgenstein ends the preface to his *Investigations* with a pronouncement of the concrete limit of his writing. Wittgenstein tells us that he cannot improve the text he had written, because time no longer permits this. However, Wittgenstein's allusion to time is concerned neither with time's objective availability nor with any chronological order of facts that could ground an understanding of why things are such and so. What Wittgenstein responds to, rather, is the unassailable presence of a concrete (or existential) impossibility that has become an important part of his life and yet bears no logical necessity and cannot even be inferred from the facts of his own biography. This impossibility does not stem from that fact or another, but grows out of the temporal unfolding of his existence, i.e., his being in time, the story of a life. In "time is past" Wittgenstein speaks of an impossibility whose internal form is the form of his entangled relationship with lived time, a relationship of which the language of the universal clock leaves no trace.

Wittgenstein's remark is reflective of its author's idiosyncratic situatedness in the very movement, the current, of a life only he can call "mine"—a situatedness whose temporal horizons are so complex and convoluted that they close in on him and shut the door for a possible future. A sense of the complexity of these concrete temporal horizons can be gleaned by rereading the preface to the *Investigations* with an eye to its internal temporal structures.

Preface

The thoughts which I publish in what follows are the precipitate of philosophical investigations that have occupied me for the last sixteen years. They concern many subjects: the concepts of meaning, of understanding, of a proposition, of logic, the foundations of mathematics, states of consciousness, and other things. I have written down all these thoughts as *remarks*. . . . It was my intention at first to bring all this together in a book whose form I pictured differently at different times. But the essential thing was that the thoughts should proceed from one subject to another in a natural order and without breaks.

After several unsuccessful attempts to weld my result together into such a whole, I realized that I should never succeed. The best that I could write would never be more than philosophical remarks; my thoughts were soon crippled if I tried to force them on in any single direction against their natural inclination.—And this was, of course , connected to the very nature of the investigation. For this compels us to travel over a wide field of thought criss-cross in every direction. The philosophical remarks in this book are, as it were, a number of sketches of landscapes which were made in the course of these long and involved journeyings. . . .

Up to a short time ago I had really given up the idea of publishing my work in my lifetime. It used, indeed, to be revived from time to time: mainly because I was obliged to learn that my results (which I communicated in lectures, typescripts and discussions), variously misunderstood, more or less mangled or watered down, were in circulation. This stung my vanity and I had difficulty quieting it.

Four years ago I had the occasion to re-read my first book (the *Tractatus Logico-Philosophicus*) and to explain its ideas to someone. It suddenly seemed to me that I should publish those old thoughts and the new ones together: that the latter could be seen in the right light only by contrast with and against the background of my old way of thinking.

For since beginning to occupy myself with philosophy again, sixteen years ago, I have been forced to recognize grave mistakes in what I wrote in that first book. I was helped to realize these mistakes ... by the criticism which my ideas encountered from Frank Ramsey, with whom I discussed them in innumerable conversations during the last two years of his life. Even more than to this ... criticism I am indebted to that which a teacher of this university, Mr. P. Sraffa, for many years unceasingly practiced on my thoughts....

For more than one reason what I publish here will have points of contact with what other people are writing today. If my remarks do not bear a stamp which marks them as mine, I do not wish to lay any further claim to them as my property.

I make them public with doubtful feelings. It is not impossible that it should fall to the lot of this work, in its poverty and in the darkness of this time, to bring light into one brain or another—but, of course, it is not likely.

I should not like my writing to spare other people the trouble of thinking. But if possible, to stimulate someone to thoughts of his own.

I should have liked to produce a good book. This has not come about, but the time is past in which I could improve it.

CAMBRIDGE
January 1945. [12]

Reading Wittgenstein's preface it is difficult not to notice the extraordinary abundance of temporal points of view, temporal modalities, and temporal shifts that are all operative in this short text. Would it be wrong to say that time itself is an issue in Wittgenstein's preface? The preface is a place where the rootedness of the *Investigations* in the experience of lived temporality is made explicit. The preface recounts a series of biographical details, facts and events, but, this biographical material would completely lose its point if we try to understand or rearrange it in the form of a linear sequence. This is because the language of the preface is one that naturally reflects the indissoluble knot by which Wittgenstein's past present and future are interrelated. Wittgenstein's language does not issue from a "now" that can be discretely located in a given chronology. The present of his utterance is not just the most recent occasion in a given series of quantifiably self-sufficient events, but is the precarious encasement of the actual passage of a life time. In this respect, Wittgenstein's preface provides a good example of how ordinary language can, in its own ways, embody the unresolved complexity of our temporal being for which, to use T. S. Eliot's lines, "time present and time past are both perhaps present in time future."

Putting this in Heideggerian terms, albeit in opposition to Heidegger's view on the ordinary, we may say that Wittgenstein's preface is a good place to begin listening to the ways in which everyday language voices the ecstatic structure of temporality. But how does the "temporalization of temporality" (as Heidegger calls it) manifest itself in language? Since we are searching here for the singular and idiosyncratic manner in which time appears in a person's language, it would be wrong, in my view, to insist on a general and unified answer to this question. The reverberation of temporality in a person's language is always concrete and singular. It cannot be identified by means of a priori criteria but requires us to develop a sensibility, an ear.

Hence, as we consider, for example, the opening sentence of Wittgenstein's preface, we may be inclined to regard its present tense, the now of the "I publish," as identical with the specific point in time, the date, that closes up the preface: "Cambridge, January 1945." However, upon a more attentive look, it becomes clear that for Wittgenstein, the "now" in which he writes his preface is clearly not a point, a mark, on the anonymous axis of time. It is not a point in a linear sequence but a voluminous moment pregnant with its past and troubled by its future. This "now" is the tip of an iceberg. It is a moment whose presence enfolds, as Wittgenstein tells us, sixteen years of philosophical investigations. These "last sixteen years" are the primary horizon of Wittgenstein's preface and it is through the evocation of this time frame that Wittgenstein's "story" begins to unfold. However, this period (roughly the years 1929–1945 in terms of clock time) does not appear to Wittgenstein as a homogeneous sequence of points, but is presented, much like a Cézanne still life, from a variety of different, not necessarily congruent, perspectives. The beginning of these last sixteen years, for example, is marked, Wittgenstein tells us, by the presence of an initial intention of lending his thoughts the form of a book. "It was my intention at first to bring all this together in a book." The intended book is envisioned as a coherent whole, but its specific form is "pictured differently at different times." Under the aegis of this governing intention, Wittgenstein makes "several unsuccessful attempts to weld [his] results together," but ultimately reaches a point of realization: "I realized that I should never succeed." Wittgenstein had wanted to write a book that would constitute a "whole," but his repeated failures lead him to the conclusion that the "best [he] could do would never be more than philosophical remarks." This realization is temporally twofold. It consists not only of Wittgenstein's understanding of his past failure but also of the totalization of this failure into the complete negation of the possibility of success in the future. Structurally similar to the preface's concluding remark, Wittgenstein's past realization is also articulated at the temporal intersection in which the now is so suffused with its past that it cannot naturally grow into the future. At the same time, however, Wittgenstein's "moment of realization" not only forces him to accept his own limitations but also brings him closer (in what was then the present) to a positive understanding of the character of his thought, his writing, and the relationship between them. That is, Wittgenstein realizes that the "very nature" of his investigation and the fragmentation constitutive of his philosophical writing are intrinsically connected. And thus, unlike his writing in the *Tractatus*, Wittgenstein no longer searches for an absolute vantage point from which the philosopher "sees the world rightly." Instead, he embraces his mature philosophical investigations as "long and involved journeyings," which open for him the sight of landscapes that cannot be viewed from an external point of view and can only be communicated further in the perspectival form of "sketches of lansdscapes"—philosophical remarks. As we continue to read the preface, however, we see that the tension between Wittgenstein's quest for totality (or his ideal of self-integration) and his incessant drive toward fragmentation is never resolved but only increases. Should we understand this apparent tension only as a symptom of Wittgenstein's struggle with philosophical writing, or is it more originally perhaps constitutive of the idiosyncratic character of his situatedness in time?

Wittgenstein's singular rapport with time cannot be mapped in a linear manner. Nevertheless, if we wish to think of the "now" in which Wittgenstein's utterance is couched with the help of an image, we may schematically represent the internal constitution of that "now" in the following way:

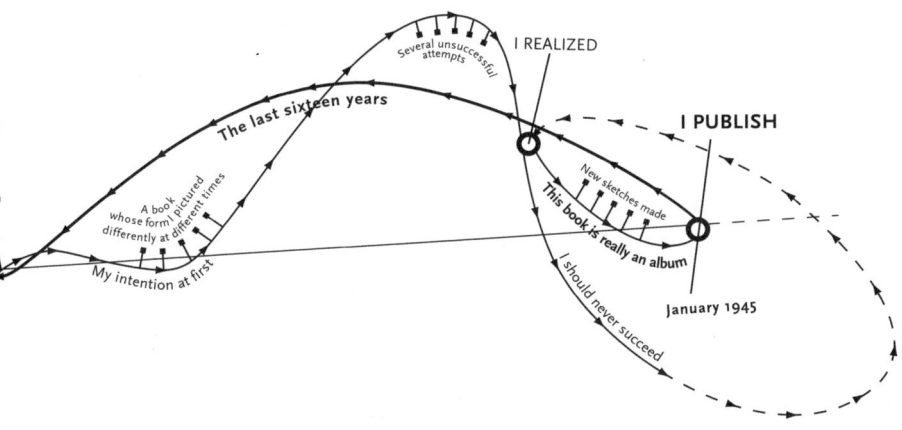

Wittgenstein's phrase "time is past" belongs to ordinary parlance. Yet, the nature of ordinary language is not as ordinary as philosophers of language seem to believe. If we engage with Wittgenstein's remark only in terms of the sentences that we can imagine ourselves saying, i.e., only on the basis of a ready-made matrix of possible meanings and forms of utterance, then we are certain to misunderstand his saying. Moreover, we shall be reproducing a form of deafness that ineluctably detemporalizes language and leaves us unresponsive to the manner in which the time of the other speaks to us. Hence, if we fail to understand how the language of the other person can possibly make room for the presence of that person's time, we are right to not understand. For there is no place for time in language. Nonetheless, there is time. Language does make time for time. And, it is our task to learn to listen to its resonance.

Another way to put this is to say that we shall remain foreign to the meaning of Wittgenstein's remark as long as we assert an identity between Wittgenstein, as a singular individual, and anyone else occupying his position. The situation of which Wittgenstein speaks is one that would not necessarily constitute an impossibility for anyone else occupying exactly that same position. In other words, the meaning of Wittgenstein's remark dissolves immediately when put in terms applicable to everyone. Moreover, the singularity of his saying will remain hidden even if we are to put ourselves "in his shoes." We cannot, in the relevant sense, be in Wittgenstein's shoes. All we can do is recognize in his familiar words the resonance of alterity.

5. In My End Is My Beginning

Today, while working on the present chapter, I was surprised to find in the bottom drawer of my desk an envelop that I thought was permanently lost. The envelop contains traces of a book I once—during an intensive year—tried and failed to write: about fifteen pages of notes and a draft of what was supposed to be the preface to that unwritten book. These pages, which, in the absence of the body of an actual book, may hardly deserve to be called a "preface," open in the following way:

> I am using the hotel's stationary for writing this preface. And writing comes as a surprise. Although I have intended for some time to return to my manuscript, I never thought that this hotel would be a place for a new beginning. I arrived yesterday. (Just) yesterday, in a big city at the end of the century, a man entered a hotel and got himself a room. Registration took longer than usual because the man insisted on a particular room on a particular floor, a room (he said)

with a specifically large window. The receptionist assured the man that the rooms in the hotel all have exactly the same size window, but in view of the man's apparent insistence, agreed to check the availability of the requested room. Yesterday, in a big city at the end of the century, I entered a hotel and checked into a room that I remember well, a room with a view.

Until a minute ago, I wanted this text to contain its beginning; I fully intended to begin from scratch, to begin at the beginning. But as I glance at these sheets of paper, the notes on the table the partly written, the already scribbled letterheads spreads around me (on the TV, the bed . . . where did I sit first?), it becomes clear that I am not in possession of my beginning, that I missed my beginning, that it started without me.

Yesterday the woman sitting next to me on the plane complained of missing the instant of departure. She said she failed to meet (or was it "greet"?) the sight of take off, failed to capture the moment she had waited for, "didn't even hear the wheels click (good-bye?)." I know her kind of disappointment: she arrived late, too late for an appointment or, in other words, she lost—what she cannot regain—a point she counted as a gain in that game she plays with time.

Her time failure is different, however, from my sense of belatedness. That is, I do not think of my late arrival as symptomatic of bad timing. Instead, it is more like the detective who is bound to appear on my TV screen in a few seconds (that's what they just said anyway, "right after the commercial break.") Violence will disrupt the order of things again and a corpse is likely to be found; the detective will examine the scene of the crime, initiate an investigation, and another episode will be underway. But why does the competent detective always arrive too late to the scene of the crime? Why does he begin only after the fact? This is not exactly a fair question. That is, within the limits of his show, the TV detective cannot ever be there on time. He cannot do what we expect him to do unless a crime has already been committed. In other words, the television episode allows the detective to go onstage and become purposeful and meaningful only after the show has already begun. This is also how I understand my own delay. My belatedness is not a slip as much as a structural condition of the work I want to be doing—(philosophy?).

I arrived late to the commencement of my text, and yet I never had the option of being on time; when I finally decided to start writing this philosophical text, I was already writing it. And, furthermore, as I attend to the last, say, twenty-four hours I spent in this room, I am unable to identify any specific moment that may be said to inaugurate this process. To put this differently, although I can recount how, upon entering the room, one thing led to another (how, for example, I suddenly had an urge to talk to you again and how, while looking for the telephone directory, I came across the hotel stationery—placed between a restaurant menu and a Bible in the dresser next to the bed—and decided that, given, the circumstances, I should probably write you a letter, a note perhaps, or even—the thought crossed my mind—just send you the hotel's letterhead in a matching envelop, just to tell you what I didn't get to say in our chance meeting yesterday, "guess where I am staying?"), these micro events are not charged with any particular intention that could substantiate—put *me* in charge of—my return to philosophy.

I should probably not dwell any further on this sense of vacuity. My time is limited, and if I really want to finish this preface before I see M. tomorrow, I have to hurry up and say whatever there is to say about . . .

Epilogue

The personal marks a certain way, a mode, of being in language. When I speak to you I may be attuned to the things you say in a personal way, and yet I may also meet your language in a manner that is impersonal. I may speak to you personally, and I might alternatively remain impersonal. The personal is a possibility. At the same time, however, the personal is also the metaphysical condition of our being in language. The personal is the root of the self's situatedness in language. One way to understand the relation between the metaphysical character and the actual possibility of the personal is to say that the essence of our situatedness in language can reveal itself to us only if we engage language in a personal manner. Another way to put this is to say that the personal essence of our being in language calls us to relate to language in a personal manner or that the basis for the ethical dimension of language is the personal essence of our being in language.

Hence the philosophical exploration of the personal is ultimately directed at uncovering the nature of the individual's being in language. In this book I have tried to show that the personal is a necessary prism for a philosophical understanding of human language, that unless we respond to the personal the phenomenon of language will remain foreign to us. Furthermore, I have argued that in order to develop a sensitivity toward the presence of the personal we need to resist the authority, the influence, and the appeal of propositional thinking. The propositional levels the personal. It altogether misplaces the possibility of listening to the personal, and it does so by objectifying language in a manner that leaves room only for an external understanding of the relationship between language and the individual. The propositional allows us to think of this relationship only after the fact of constructing language and the individual as two independent, fully constituted, entities. As we've seen, however, the externality of the relationship between the individual and language is symptomatic not only of the philosophical tendency to internalize the hegemony of the propositional but also of the opposite tendency to struggle against this hegemony. Language's external relation to the individual is symptomatic of the philosophical tendency to subsume the existence of the individual to language's public form of intelligibility. But it is equally characteristic of the tendency to present the individual in opposition to that form of intelligibility.

In this book I have tried to open up the question of the relationship between the speaking subject and her language in a new way. This was done by showing that the meeting of language and individuality is itself an important and enigmatic phenomenon that typically escapes philosophy's ears: this is the place of the individual's attachment to language, a place that is typically concealed by the prototypical investigation of the workings of language. What has concerned us here, in other words, are neither the representational (e.g., epistemic) nor the instrumental (e.g., intentional) aspects of a person's successful use of language but rather a more fundamental level of involvement, or fusion, that exists between language and the self.

In this sense, the present study is an attempt to uncover for philosophy a deep and genuine question. This is the question of the intimate character of the attachment, of the being-with and being-in by which the individual and language are related.

We have seen how natural it is for philosophical reflection to remain indifferent to the phenomenality of this being-in, however. And have consequently called for a phenomenology of the tension between the individual and her language. It is in this tension that the personal is present. This tension is where the personal lives.

Hence the primary concern of this book is to uncover the irreducible presence of the personal and to develop a philosophical ear for the resonance of this marriage between the singularity of existence and the public structure or the ordinary form of the intelligible. In particular, I have suggested that once we recognize the personal the possibility opens for us to begin to listen to language as the embodiment of the unique, idiosyncratic presence of the speaking individual. In this study I have only taken the first steps toward—only opened the horizons for—a phenomenology of this enigmatic fusion. How can the general, abstract, and public form of language provide an actual home for a person's concrete existence? What exactly does it mean to listen to spoken language as the embodiment of a speaker's singularity? In what sense can language be said to embody the individual's singular existence?

We have arrived at the end of this study. And at this point, where I can only gesture toward those avenues that invite further investigation, let me try to touch upon the crux of the questions that I leave open by considering a Hasidic tale told by Rabbi Nachman of Bratslav: the tale of the prince who took himself to be a turkey.[1] There was once a prince who, according to Rabbi Nachman, took ill and became convinced that he was a big bird, something of a turkey. Stripping off his clothes, the naked prince refused to interact with his fellow men and insisted on dwelling under the royal dinning table, pecking crumbs off the floor. Most worried, the king summoned the best and most famous doctors of the land to the palace, but none were able to cure the prince. Deeply saddened by the condition of his son and concerned about the future of his kingdom, the king began to sink into despair. It was, thus, quite a surprise when a wise man arrived at the palace one day and offered to heal the prince.

Entering the royal dinning room, the wise man immediately took off his clothes and sat down naked under the table next to the prince. "Who are you and what are you doing here?" the prince asked the wise man, who was already busy pecking crumbs off the floor. "And what are you doing here?" responded the wise man with a question. "I am a turkey," the prince answered. "So am I," said the wise man, and the two continued to sit there under the table.

As time passed and the two turkeys became accustomed to each other's presence, the wise man gave a signal to the king's servants to bring some garments and place them under the table. When the wise man then donned a shirt, the alarmed prince asked, "Why are you doing that? I thought you said you're a turkey!" The wise man replied that there's nothing wrong with being a turkey and wearing a shirt; wearing a shirt doesn't make you any less of a turkey. "Of course I'm a turkey," he said. "Why should wearing a shirt change that fact? I am a turkey who simply wishes to put on a shirt. Would you like to see how it feels to put one on yourself?" The prince agreed to try. After a while the wise man suggested they also attempt to wear trousers. Again the wise man asked the prince why he thought that wearing trousers should be opposed to their identities as turkeys. The prince acceded, and, now comfortably dressed, the two turkeys continued their life under the table.

When the wise man signaled the king's servants to place some of the royal chef's most delectable dishes on the floor, the prince vehemently objected. But, once again, the wise man convinced the prince that one does not cease being a turkey just because he eats fine food. "Why can't you be the turkey you are while eating a good meal?" As time passed, the wise man introduced the prince to a rich horizon of possibilities open to turkeys such as himself: eating while sitting at the table, using silverware and china, adopting table manners, engaging others socially, and, finally, even attending to the affairs of the kingdom.

For Rabbi Nachman of Bratslav, the wise man's curing of the prince serves as an allegory for the possibility of helping those who are lost to find their own individual way back to God. But, for our purposes, what makes this tale particularly relevant is that it allows us to elaborate a view on language by which we may resist the common opposition between the private, idiosyncratic, place of the speaking individual and the general, public structure of the intelligible.

The basic setting of the story is, as suggested, the prince's "condition." The prince has changed, and this metamorphosis is unsettling for his surrounding. The prince's transformation is particularly disturbing because it fractures the shared grounds, the commonality, of meaning that was, up to that point, completely taken for granted. The possibility of communicating with the prince seems to be no longer available. And, in the palace, this sudden collapse of the usual structures of communicability is immediately interpreted as a sign of the prince's illness, his aberrance or abnormality. In other words, the failure of those standard forms of communication to sustain a shared sense of the world is understood in terms of the relationship between the inside and the outside of a (seemingly) cohesive "we" for which the world continues to be simply what it is. Hence, for the king and his staff, the transformed prince is an outsider, an alien, who has ceased to belong to their community of the "we." The attempts to cure the prince are all based on this opposition between the ordinary meaningfulness of the world and the prince's radically idiosyncratic condition. The cure for which the famous, albeit unsuccessful, doctors are searching is thus one that would consist in the elimination of the essence of strangeness that seems to exclude the prince from the domain of "our" normal human world. The doctors labor to bring the prince back into the familiar abode of ordinary everydayness. And this, they think, would be possible only by overcoming, by canceling out, the idiosyncratic singularity of the prince's self-understanding. Moreover, we may note that the dichotomous presuppositions governing the palace's response are ultimately shared also by the prince himself. That is, he too operates with the conviction that his new identity as a turkey is constituted in—and through the—opposition to that human "we."

The wise man sees things differently and, to begin with, resists the appeal of any binary conception of the situation. The path he takes is dialogical at heart. Dialogue provides the horizons of his engagement with the prince, and it is his faith in the possibility of having a dialogue with the prince that allows him to proceed with the healing. For the wise man, the ostensible alterity of the prince—the deep rift that has opened up in between the prince and his community—does not stand in the way of a mutual understanding. The wise man seeks to reintegrate the prince into the public domain of human intelligibility, but he does not envision the ideal of shared meaning as exclusive, in any way, of the prince's core of alterity.

The wise man leads the prince back to the meaningfulness of ordinary everydayness. He enables the prince to return to his position as a prince without having to lose or renounce his identity as a turkey. Instead of struggling against the prince's birdlike predilections, the wise man teaches the prince how to embrace the ordinary together with these idiosyncratic aspects of his existence. That is, he helps the prince to find his home again in the common domain of human meaning but, at the same time, allows the prince to preserve that singularity that makes him a complete stranger.

The story ends with the return of the prince to the ordinary: the prince is cured and is fully fit to participate again in the kingdom's affairs. But despite the happy resolution of the plot, the tale's ending subverts the possibility of ever returning to a simple and homogeneous form of everydayness. The prince is cured. For his surrounding, his illness is a matter of the past—a passing illness. His position in the public sphere is completely restored. The prince is a prince is a prince. But we, as readers of the tale, cannot ignore the fact that the prince continues to experience the world from the perspective of a big bird. What does this mean? The tale invites us to recognize that the prince's mode of being in language is ultimately no different from our own. It invites us to see how the presence of a person's idiosyncratic singularity can silently, yet thoroughly, pervade—cut through, carve itself into—the public form of his or her meaningfulness. The story of the prince encourages us to question the self-sameness and uniformity grounding our public sphere of meaning. And it does so by suggesting that the singularity of existence is operative and effective in the generation of a person's speech, creating an invisible center of gravity that inflects the whole universe of his or her language. The phenomenon of spoken language is thus neither uniform nor average because its horizons in each individual case are bent or molded in an individual way.

To listen to the personal is to be open to the resonance of an irresolvable tension in a person's language. This is a tension between, on the one hand, the public uniformity of a person's words—the words of a prince—and, on the other hand, the utterly private roots these words have in the world of a turkey. The personal is an unexpected fusion between prince and turkey that is heard in my language, if you only care to listen. Is this you?

Notes

Introduction: Philosophy and the Personal

1. Robert Brandom, *Making It Explicit* (Cambridge: Harvard University Press, 1994), p. 67.
2. Ibid., p. 4.
3. Ibid., p. 5.
4. John McDowell, "Meaning, Communication, and Knowledge," in *Meaning, Knowledge, and Reality* (Cambridge: Harvard University Press, 1998), pp. 39, 45.
5. Maurice Blanchot, "Studies On Language," in *Faux Pas*, trans. C. Mandell (Stanford: Stanford University Press, 2001), p. 89.
6. When Foucault, for example, writes that "we now know that the being of language is the visible effacement of the one who speaks," his position echoes the Nietzschean insight that "words depersonalize;" however, whereas for Nietzsche the averageness and herd quality of language is a predicament that a genuine individual must struggle against, Foucault's explicit agenda is altogether to rid our understanding of discourse of that gravitational center which the individual subject traditionally occupies. See Michel Foucault, "Maurice Blanchot: The Thought from Outside," in *Foucault, Blanchot*, trans. Brian Massumi (New York: Zone, 1990), p.54; Friedrich Nietzsche, *The Gay Science*, trans. Walter Kaufmann (New York: Vintage, 1974), §354. The personal is thus not just overlooked by much of the more contemporary work done in the continental tradition, but is actually criticized, not the least by Foucault, Derrida, Deleuze, and even Levinas.

7. Martin Heidegger, *Being and Time*, trans. J. Macquarrie and E. Robinson (New York: Harper and Row, 1962), p. 165.
8. Heidegger, *Being and Time*, p. 167.
9. Herbert Marcuse, *One Dimensional Man* (London: Routledge and Kegan Paul, 1970), p. 140.
10. Ibid.
11. Ibid.
12. J. P. Sartre, *Being and Nothingness*, trans. H. Barnes (New York: Philosophical Library, 1966), p. 372.
13. Blanchot, "Studies on Language," p. 190.
14. Ibid.

1. Language and the Bell Jar

1. Ludwig Wittgenstein, *Philosophical Investigations*, trans. G. E. M. Anscombe (Oxford: Basil Blackwell, 1984), §115, p. 48.
2. Cartesianism can serve as a good example, in this context, of a picture whose influence is often propagated in a manner that does not have to do with the question of whether we agree with Descartes or not. Despite Descartes's explicit appeal to reason, it is, in fact, the imagination that his texts have proved to deeply affect. And thus, having rejected practically each and every thesis expounded by Descartes—having lain his claims behind, exposing their flaws and inadequacies—we may nevertheless remain captives of his thought, if our philosophical imagination is still Cartesian. On Descartes and the space of metaphor, see Hagi Kenaan, "The Philosopher and the Window," in *Descartes: Reception and Disenchantment*, ed. Y. Senderowicz and Y. Wahl (Tel Aviv: Tel Aviv University Publishing Projects, 2000), pp.195–208.
3. Wittgenstein, *Investigations*, §109, p.47.
4. Ibid., §114, p. 48.
5. Ibid., §104, p.46.
6. Aristotle, *De Interpretatione*, trans. J. L. Ackrill in *Categories and De Interpretatione*, ed. J. L. Ackrill (Oxford: Oxford University Press, 1990), 16b33.
7. Bertrand Russell, "Introduction" to Wittgenstein's *Tractatus Logico-Philosophicus* (London: Routledge, 1981), p.8.
8. See, for example, John McDowell, "Meaning, Communication, and Knowledge," in *Meaning, Knowledge, and Reality* (Cambridge: Harvard University Press, 1998), p. 39.
9. Bertrand Russell, *An Inquiry Into Meaning and Truth*, (London: George Allen and Unwin, 1950), p. 30.
10. Donald Davidson, "The Method of Truth in Metaphysics," in *Inquiries Into Truth and Interpretation* (Oxford: Oxford University Press, 1984), p. 201.

2. THE LIMITS OF LANGUAGE AND THE DREAM OF TRANSCENDENCE 185

11. Robert Brandom, *Making it Explicit* (Cambridge: Harvard University Press, 1994), p. 173. For Brandom, assertion is the fundamental speech act because it is "what distinguishes a practice as specifically linguistic.... It is only because some performances function as assertions that others deserve to be distinguished as *speech* acts" (172).
12. See, for example, ibid., p. 79–80: "It is appropriate to begin by addressing propositional contents because of what can be called the *pragmatic priority of the propositional.*" For Brandom, the basic epistemic insight underlying the priority of the propositional can be traced back to one of Kant's "cardinal innovations . . . that the fundamental unit of awareness or cognition, the minimum graspable, is the *judgement.*"
13. Friedrich Nietzsche, *The Will to Power*, trans. W. Kaufman and R. Holligdale (New York: Random House, 1969), §481.
14. Although positivism has been out of fashion for a long time, and there are no philosophers today who would want to present themselves or their projects as positivistic, Nietzsche's characterization of the positivistic position remains highly relevant to the contemporary debate.
15. Hence, Brandom, for example, emphasizes that whereas "facts are what make claiming true . . . talk of facts as what makes claims true is confused if it is thought of as relating two distinct things—a true claim and the fact in virtue of which it is true." For him, rather, "the claim that 'p is true' and 'it is a fact that p' are two equivalent ways of saying the same thing—expressing the same content, and so (if the claim they both express is true) stating the same fact" (328). In other words, while Brandom contends that "the world is everything that is the case, a constellation of facts," he also underscores the need of "giving up the picture of how things are as contrasting with what we can say and think. Facts are (the contents) of true claims and thoughts" (333).
16. Bertrand Russell, "The Philosophy of Logical Atomism," in *Logic and Knowledge: Essays 1901–1950* (New York: Capricorn, 1971), p. 182.
17. Donald Davidson, "True to the Facts," in *Inquiries Into Truth and Interpretation* (Oxford: Oxford University Press, 1984), p. 49.
18. Plato, *Sophist, Collected Dialogues of Plato*, trans. F. M. Cornford, ed. E. Hamilton and H. Cairns (Princeton: Princeton University Press, 1982), 262d.

2. The Limits of Language and the Dream of Transcendence

1. Søren Kierkegaard, *Either/Or*, trans. D. Swenson and L. M. Swenson (Princeton: Princeton University Press, 1959), 1:31.
2. Søren Kierkegaard, *Concluding Unscientific Postscript*, trans. D. Swenson (Princeton: Princeton University Press, 1985), p. 267.
3. For a different perspective on philosophy and disappointment see Simon

2. THE LIMITS OF LANGUAGE AND THE DREAM OF TRANSCENDENCE

Critchley, *Very Little . . . Almost Nothing: Death, Philosophy, Literature* (New York: Routledge, 1997), pp. 2–3.
4. Kierkegaard, *Concluding Unscientific Postscript*, p. 267.
5. Ibid., p. 279.
6. John McDowell, "Meaning, Communication, and Knowledge," in *Meaning, Knowledge, and Reality* (Cambridge: Harvard University Press, 1998), pp. 39, 45.
7. Søren Kierkegaard, *Fear and Trembling*, trans. H. Hong and E. Hong (Princeton: Princeton University Press, 1983), p. 55. Page references will hereafter appear parenthetically in text.
8. Czeslaw Milosz, "Dedication," in *The Collected Poems, 1931–1987* (New York: Ecco, 1988), p. 78.
9. B. F. McGuinness, ed., *Ludwig Wittgenstein and the Vienna Circle: Conversations Recorded by Friedrich Waismann* (Oxford: Blackwell, 1979), p. 69.
10. For a discussion of the meaning of anamorphosis and the secret of Holbein's *Ambassadors*, see, Hagi Kenaan, "The Unusual Character of Holbein's Ambassadors," *Artibus et Historiae* 46 (23): 61–75.
11. Franz Kafka, "Before the Law," in *The Complete Stories*, ed. N. Glatzer (New York: Schoken, 1971), pp. 3–4.
12. Bertrand Russell, "Introduction" to Wittgenstein's *Tractatus Logico-Philosophicus* (London: Routledge 1981), p. 8.
13. Kafka, "Before the Law," p. 4.
14. Kierkegaard, *Either/Or*, p. 31.

3. Austin's Fireworks

1. J. L. Austin, *How to Do Things with Words*, ed. J. O. Urmson and M. Sbisa (Cambridge: Harvard University Press, 1962), p. 149. Austin draws here five morals, of which only the first two will concern us.
2. Ibid., p. 164. For Austin, however this means that he has "been sorting out a bit of the way things have already begun to go and are going with increasing momentum in some parts of philosophy, rather than proclaiming an individual manifesto."
3. In "A Plea for Excuses," for example, Austin expresses his reluctance to regard his own philosophical work as an instance of "ordinary language philosophy" and his suspicion "of such names as 'linguistic' or 'analytic' philosophy, or 'the analysis of language.'" His preference, rather, is for "some less misleading name than those given above—for instance, 'linguistic phenomenology.'" See J. L. Austin, "A Plea for Excuses," in *Philosophical Papers* (Oxford: Oxford University Press, 1961), p. 130.
4. Peter Strawson, "Meaning and Truth," in *Logico Linguistic Papers* (London: Methuen, 1971), p. 189.
5. See, for example, A. P. Martinich, ed., *The Philosophy of Language* (Oxford:

Oxford University Press, 1990), p. 103: "Austin presented a tentative ... theory of speech acts in *How to Do Things with Words*. John Searle substantially revised that theory and presented what has since become the standard theory in *Speech Acts*."

6. John Searle, *Speech Acts: An Essay in the Philosophy of Language* (Cambridge: Cambridge University Press, 1968), p. 31.
7. "We can then symbolize different kinds of illocutionary acts in the form, e.g., -(p) for assertions, !(p) for requests, Pr(p) for promise, W(p) for warnings, ?(p) for yes-no questions, and so on." Searle, *Speech Acts*, p. 31.
8. See, for example, Brandom's *Making It Explicit*, p.187: "It requires ... that the significance of a speech act depends in a systematic way on the content and the sort of force that is attached to it."
9. John McDowell, "Truth Conditions, Bivalence and Verificationism," in *Truth and Meaning*, ed. G. Evans and J. McDowell (Oxford: Clarendon Press, 1976), p.45.
10. John McDowell, "On the Sense and Reference of a Proper Name," *Mind* 86.342 (1977): 166.
11. For example, Robert Brandom, *Making It Explicit* (Cambridge: Harvard University Press, 1994), p. 83: "The theoretical point of attributing semantic content to intentional states, attitudes, and performances is to determine the pragmatic significance of their occurrence in various contexts. This means settling how linguistic expressions of those contents are properly or correctly used. ... It is specifically *propositional* contents that determine these pragmatic significances, so it is specifically propositional contents that it is the task of semantic explanatory theories to attribute."
12. Austin, *How to Do Things with Words*, p. 1. Subsequent references appear in text.
13. "Grammarians have not, I believe, seen through this 'disguise,' and philosophers only at best incidentally." Ibid., p. 4.
14. Reading *How to Do Things with Words*, it is clear from the very start not only that Austin has an interest in the pragmatic dimension of language but that his basic motivation for dealing with the performative is a pragmatic one as well. Yet it is not until lecture 7 that pragmatic tendencies become explicit. That is, it is only after an explicit discrediting of the semantic conception of the linguistic field that the speech act becomes thematized.
15. Gottlob Frege's sedimental work can serve as a good illustration of the unreflective tendency to posit such an identity. Frege, for example, finds it completely natural to posit the declarative sentence as the ultimate standard for, and the essential *explanandum* of, philosophical analysis of language. In "Sense and Reference," in *Translations from the Philosophical Writings*, trans. P. Geach and M. Black (Oxford: Oxford University Press,

1977), he writes: "We now inquire concerning the sense and referent of an entire declarative sentence. Such a sentence contains a thought." (62).
16. See, for example, Martin Heidegger, *Being and Time*, §33.
17. Jurgen Habermas, "Social Action, Purposive Activity, and Communication," in *On the Pragmatics of Communication* (Cambridge: MIT Press, 1998), p. 128.
18. Jurgen Habermas, "Actions, Speech Acts, Linguistically Mediated Interaction, and the Lifeworld," in *On the Pragmatics of Communication*, p. 219.
19. On the role of success and the place of failure in the context of Derrida's and Searle's conflicting readings of Austin, see Hagi Kenaan, "Language, Philosophy, and the Risk of Failure: Rereading the Debate Between Searle and Derrida," *Continental Philosophy Review* 35.2 (June 2002): 117–133.
20. Ludwig Wittgenstein, *Philosophical Investigations*, trans. G. E. M. Anscombe (Oxford: Basil Blackwell, 1984), §415.
21. See, for example, ibid., §23: "The speaking of language is part of an activity, or a form of life."

4. Personal Objects

1. Martin Heidegger, *Being and Time*, trans. J. Macquarrie and E. Robinson (New York: Harper and Row, 1962), p. 203. Subsequent page references to this work will appear parenthetically in text.
2. Heidegger, "Dialogue on Language," in *On the Way to Language*, trans. P. D. Hertz (New York: Harper and Row, 1982), p. 41.
3. J. L. Austin, *How to Do Things with Words*, ed. J. O. Urmson and M. Sbisa (Cambridge: Harvard University Press, 1962), p. 149.
4. Heidegger, "The Nature of Language," in *On the Way to Language*, p. 59.
5. Heidegger, "Language," in *Poetry, Language, Thought*, trans. A. Hofstadter (New York: Harper and Row, 1971), p. 189.
6. This leads Heidegger to characterize the work of "linguists and philologists of the most diverse language, psychologists and analytic philosophers" as primarily concerned with the gathering of "information about language." They "supply [information] to us, and constantly increase the supply, *ad infinitum*." Furthermore, according to him, "the scientific and philosophical investigation of languages is aiming ever more resolutely at the production of what is called a 'metalanguage.' Analytical philosophy, which is set on producing this super-language, is thus quite consistent when it considers itself metalinguistics. . . . Metalinguistics is the metaphysics of the thoroughgoing technicalization of all languages into the sole operative instrument of interplanetary information." And since "scientific and philosophical information about language" is the constitutive and regulating *telos* of the scientific and philosophical investigation

of language, these forms of investigation are seen by Heidegger to be a symptom of technology's global homogenization of the field of meaning. As Heidegger puts it, "language and Sputnik, metalinguistics and rocketry are the Same." Heidegger, "The Nature of Language," p. 58.
7. In this respect, Heidegger's poetic or aesthetic turn toward language—his insistence on poetry as the "original" locus of "what is spoken purely"—is not a simple negation of the propositional but a second-order response based on an understanding of the propositional as the outcome of a problematic appropriation of the pragmatic. Accordingly, Heidegger's poetic alternative should be understood, not only as a way of countering the propositional, but, first of all, as an attempt to overcome the pragmatic.
8. Heidegger, "The Nature of Language," p. 57.
9. Heidegger, "On the Way to Language," in *On the Way to Language*, p. 119.
10. Heidegger, "Language," p.194.
11. Heidegger, "The Nature of Language," p. 59.
12. Heidegger, "On the Way to Language," p. 131.
13. Heidegger, "Language," p. 195.
14. Martin Heidegger, "The Origin of the Work of Art," in *Poetry, Language, Thought*, trans. A. Hofstadter (New York: Harper and Row, 1971), p. 35. References will hereafter appear parenthetically in text.
15. Meyer Schapiro, "The Still Life as a Personal Object—A Note on Heidegger and van Gogh," in *Selected Papers, Theory and Philosophy of Art: Style, Artist, and Sociey* (New York: Braziller, 1994), 4:138.
16. W. J. T. Mitchell, "Schapiro's Legacy," *Art in America* 83 (April 1995): 29.
17. Jacques Derrida, "Restitutions" in *The Truth in Painting*, trans. G. Bennington and I. McLeod (Chicago: University of Chicago Press, 1987). For Derrida, the lesson of the dispute between the two thinkers is completely negative. Focusing on the senses in which Schapiro's critique of Heidegger reproduces Heidegger misuse of van Gogh's painting, Derrida mocks the very attempt to identify a referent for van Gogh's painting, and moves to deconstruct the "pair-image" that dominates both readings of van Gogh. According to Derrida, the conceptualization of the shoes as a pair only testifies to the fact that both thinkers are still caught in a metaphysical—modernistic—picture of a subject.
18. Mitchell, "Schapiro's Legacy," p. 29.
19. The question of the place and status of the visual in Heidegger's *Being and Time* cannot be dealt with here. For a discussion of Heidegger's "hostility" toward the visual, see for example, Martin Jay's *Downcast Eyes: the Denigration of Vision in Twentieth-Century French Thought* (Berkeley: University of California Press, 1994), pp. 263–275. For an interesting critique of Heidegger's analysis of curiosity—intrinsically associated with sight—see Karsten Harries, "Truth and Freedom" in *Studies in Philosophy and the*

History of Philosophy (Washington: Catholic University of America Press, 1981), 18:131–155.
20. On the place of looking in philosophy and the relationship between the visual, the textual, and the ethical in "The Origin of the Work of Art," see Hagi Kenaan, "What Philosophy Owes a Work of Art: Rethinking the Debate Between Heidegger and Schapiro," *Symposium: Canadian Journal of Continental Philosophy* 8 (Fall 2004): 3
21. For a discussion of Heidegger's misuse of his philosophical authority in his treatment of poetry,and in particular, in his choice of Hölderlin as his hero, see Karsten Harries, "The Root of All Evil: Lessons of an Epigram," *International Journal of Philosophical Studies* 1.1 (March 1993): 1–20.
22. Milan Kundera, *The Unbearable Lightness of Being*, trans. M. H. Heim (New York: Harper and Row, 1984), p. 61. Further references to this work will appear parenthetically in text.
23. Wittgenstein, *Philosophical Investigations*, §527.
24. Bertolt Brecht, "Pleasures," in *Poems 1913–1956*, trans. M. Hamburger, ed. J. Willett and R. Manheim (New York: Methuen, 1976), p. 448.

5. Language Unframed: Beauty as a Model

1. All examples are from Robert Brandom, *Making It Explicit* (Cambridge: Harvard University Press, 1994).
2. We need to see that what you were saying belongs to the kind of speech—to a range of linguistic fluctuations—that philosophy usually fails to hear, and that this failure has to do, first of all, with philosophy's imprisonment in the propositional, but also with the two central ways philosophy actually tries to overcome the propositional, by a turn to the pragmatic or to the poetic.
3. Ludwig Wittgenstein, *Philosophical Investigations*, trans. G. E. M. Anscombe (Oxford: Basil Blackwell, 1984), §114.
4. The space of reason within which subjective utterances operate, for example, often seems to make room for distinctive asymmetries between our self-understanding—our access to ourselves—and our understanding of the external world (e.g., subjective language makes room for a logic of implicature that cannot always be generalized into, and is not directly derived from, the ways we speak of our shared world).
5. Of course, one cannot begin to answer such questions unless one first learns more about the circumstances of your utterance. In philosophical considerations of language this is something that is hardly done, because of the tendency to think of language independently of the folds of the stories—and there's always a story, a story rather than a context—through which this phenomenon shows itself. But the point I wish to make here is not about how to decide between the objective and subjective interpre-

tation of your utterance. It is about the implications—in my view, the problematic implications—that both of these two interpretations commit us to.

6. Immanuel Kant, *Critique of Judgment*, trans. W. S. Pluhar (Indianapolis: Hackett, 1987), p. 7. References will hereafter appear parenthetically in text.
7. Austin, of course, has no interest in the aesthetic dimension of language, but his pragmatic shift undermines the apparent homogeneity of the space of language and reveals the presence of a rich and heterogeneous fabric of language underlying the representative cover of fact-depiction.
8. J. L. Austin, *How to Do Things with Words*, ed. J. O. Urmson and M. Sbisa (Cambridge: Harvard University Press, 1962), p. 4.
9. Edmund Husserl, *Ideas: A General Introduction to Pure Phenomenology*, trans. W. R. Boyce Gibson (New York: Collier Macmillan, 1962), p. 92.

6. Personal Time

1. See, for example, Maurice Merleau-Ponty, "Eye and Mind," in *The Primacy of Perception*, trans. J. Edie (Evanston: Northwestern University Press, 1964), p.162: "The Painter takes his body with him, says Valery. Indeed we cannot imagine how a *mind* could paint. It is by lending his body to the world that the artist changes the world into paintings. To understand these transubstitutions we must go back to the working, actual body . . . which is an intertwining of vision and movement."
2. Ludwig Wittgenstein, *Philosophical Investigations*, trans. G. E. M. Anscombe (Oxford: Basil Blackwell, 1984), p. viii.
[Ich hätte gerne ein gutes Buch hervorgebracht. Es ist nicht so ausgefallen; aber die Zeit ist vorbei, in der es von mir verbessert werden könnte].
3. Wittgenstein concludes the preface to his *Tractatus*, as follows:
If the work has value it consists of two things. First that in it thoughts are expressed, and this value will be greater the better the thoughts are expressed. The more the nail has been hit on the head. Here I am conscious that I have fallen far short of the possible. Simply because my powers are insufficient to cope with the task. May others come and do it better. On the other hand, the truth of the thoughts seems to me unassailable and definitive. I am therefore of the opinion that the problems have in essentials been finally solved. And if I am not mistaken, then the value of this work secondly consists in the fact that it shows how little has been done when these problems have been solved." Ludwig Wittgenstein, *Tractatus Logico-Philosophicus*, trans. C. K. Ogden (London: Routledge, 1981), p. 29.
For a stimulating discussion of the relationship of philosophy and autobiography in Wittgenstein's *Tractatus*, see, Eli Friedlander, *Signs of*

4. Henry Bergson, *Matter and Memory*, trans. N. M. Paul and W. S. Palmer (London: George Allen and Unwin, 1962), p.194.
5. The scope of this chapter does not allow me to develop the question of time independently of the question of language. However, the philosophical insight that motivates my critique of a propositional language of time can be found (in different versions) in phenomenological-existential accounts of temporality, from Husserl to Heidegger to Merleau-Ponty. As is probably clear, my primary debt goes to Heidegger's work on temporality from which, however, I ultimately part ways. This is because for Heidegger, the elision of the ecstatic structure of Dasein's temporality is symptomatic of everyday language that can only reflect the averageness of everyday experience ruled by the anonymity of *das Man*. See Martin Heidegger, *Being and Time*, trans. J. Macquarrie and E. Robinson (New York: Harper and Row, 1962), division 2. See also Martin Heidegger, *The Basic Problems of Phenomenology*, trans. A. Hofstadter (Bloomington: Indiana University Press, 1988), part 2.
6. Wittgenstein, *Tractatus*, p. 189, §6.54.
7. René Descartes, *The Philosophical Writings of Descartes*, trans. J. Cottingham, R. Stootgoff, and D. Murdoch (Cambridge: Cambridge University Press, 1990), 2:12.
8. Immanuel Kant, *Critique of Judgment*, trans. W. S. Pluhar (Indianapolis: Hackett, 1987), pp. 7–8.
9. Heidegger, "Author's Preface to the Seventh German Audition," in *Being and Time*, p. xvii.
10. W. V. O. Quine, "Preface to the Revised Edition," in *The Pursuit of Truth* (Cambridge: Harvard University Press, 1992).
11. W. V. O. Quine, *Word and Object* (Cambridge: MIT Press, 1960), p. 158. Subsequent references appear parenthetically in text.
12. Wittgenstein, *Philosophical Investigations*, p. vii.

Epilogue

1. Rabbi Nachman of Bratslav, "The Tale of the Prince Who Took Himself to Be a Turkey," in *The Writings of Rabbi Nachman of Bratslav* [Hebrew], ed. Eliezer Steinmann (Tel Aviv: Knesset Tel Aviv, 1955), pp. 157–158.

Index

Abraham (biblical), 50–52
Abstraction, language of, 45
Acknowledgment, 147
Aesthetics, 135–38
Affect: of individuality, 9; meaning of pictures and, 21
Alienation, 99
Alterity, 174, 181
Anglo-American philosophy, 1, 2, 66; content and, 9, 12; everyday language and, 126; hegemony of the propositional in, 8, 27, 87, 88–89, 95, 134, 140; Heidegger and, 94; on language and human interaction, 81; on logical necessity and truth, 49; pragmatic turn and, 87; structure of information, 8; *see also* Philosophy of language
Anxiety, 97
Aristotle, *De Interpretatione*, 27
Austin, J. L., 16, 26, 65, 87; Heidegger compared with, 91–94, 96; *How to Do Things with Words*, 65, 66, 69, 71, 72, 74, 75, 77, 187n14; language's situatedness and, 91; linguistic interaction and, 80–82; performativity and, 139, 140; philosophical tradition and, 71; pragmatic form and, 66–69, 70, 80, 82, 96; propositional form and, 83; on speech act, 72–79
Authenticity, 12, 15, 48–49, 96

Bad faith, 127
Beauty, 136–38, 140, 141, 142
Being-in-the-world, 95, 131, 141
Bergson, Henri, 155, 167
Blanchot, Maurice, 10, 15
Brandom, Robert, 7, 28; *Making It Explicit*, 7, 187n11, 190n1
Brecht, Bertolt: *Last Poems*, 122; "Pleasures," 122–23

Captivity, 20–24, 36, 43, 54, 89, 111–12
Cézanne, Paul, 127, 172
Chronology, 165, 166–68

Communication, 15, 28, 80, 99; "communication poles," 32, 143; everydayness and, 115; existence and, 121–22; failure of standard forms of, 180–81; force and, 70; indirect, 53
Comte, August, 29
Conscience, 96–97
Constative sentences, 73, 74, 75, 76, 139
Content, 8, 12, 78, 91; authentic communication and, 15; content and the personal, 149–50; everyday language as reflection, 22; as limiting factor, 16–17; propositional structure of, 9, 28, 79, 121; self-identity and, 33; speech and, 83
Continental philosophy, 1, 2, 66; everyday language and, 126; experience of individuality and, 10; hegemony of the propositional and, 121; on logical necessity and truth, 49; model of ordinary language, 13; structural limits of language and, 14
Creativity, 115, 120

Dasein, 11–12, 90, 92–94, 97, 162; being-in-the-world of, 95; "they-self" and, 145; uprootedness and, 96
Davidson, Donald, 28
Deleuze, Gilles, 183*n*6
Derrida, Jacques, 9, 12, 106, 126, 189*n*17
Descartes, René, 161–63, 184*n*1:2; Cartesian epistemology, 66, 184*n*1:2; *Meditations*, 161–63
Desire, 116
Dialogue, 181
Disappointment, 41, 42–43, 60–63

Eliot, T. S., 116, 171
Emotions, 57, 130, 145
Epistemology, 66
Equipmentality (instrumentality), 103, 104, 108, 116
Eroticism, 141
Ethics, 5, 177
Euryclea, 17
Everydayness (the ordinary), 15–16, 98–99, 182; poetry of, 121, 122–23; as prison, 95–97
Exercitives, 81
Existence, 43, 45, 48, 121–22, 179
Existentialism, 10, 16; *see also* Heidegger, Martin; Kierkegaard, Søren; Sartre, Jean-Paul
Expressivity, 130

Face, human, 4–5, 23
Facts, 29–32, 59, 80; constative sentences, 73, 74; existence and, 49; intelligibility and, 156; irrelevance of, 109; language's structure and, 121; possibility and, 154, 155; speech act and, 83; suchness of things and, 38
Falsehood, 27, 28, 31; expressivity and, 130; performatives and, 74; philosophy as disappointment and, 42–43; suchness of things and, 129
Foucault, Michel, 183*n*6
Freedom, 16, 20, 56, 57, 60, 63; everydayness as captivity and, 111–12; facts and, 121; hegemony of the propositional and, 88; structure versus, 4, 54
Frege, Gottlob, 21, 187*n*15
Freud, Sigmund, 12
Functionality, 69, 90–95

Gaze, 22, 113, 114, 119, 144
Generality, 43, 49

INDEX   195

Good life, 42
Grammar, 75, 76, 129

Habermas, Jürgen, 80–81
Happiness, 42
Harries, Karsten, 190n21
Hegel, Georg Wilhelm Friedrich, 10, 11
Hegelian system, 11
Heidegger, Martin, 3, 9, 15, 26, 52, 84; *Being and Time*, 11–12, 89, 90–91, 95, 97, 98, 103, 109, 119, 141, 161, 162, 164–65; on Dasein and "they-self," 11–12, 96, 145; on intelligibility and the personal, 88–95; limits of language and, 53–54; on logos, 19, 35–36; on metalanguage, 188–89n6; "Nature of Language, The," 100; on the ordinary as prison, 95–97; "Origin of the Work of Art," 87, 102, 108–9, 110; the personal and, 97–102; philosophical preface and, 161, 162, 164–65; poetry and, 100, 101–2, 189n7; pragmatic interpretation of the ordinary, 90–95; on temporality, 171, 192n5; on time, 164–65; on truth, 87, 121; on Van Gogh painting of shoes, 102–11, 112; "What Is Metaphysics," 52
Heraclitus, 19, 117
Holbein, Hans: *Ambassadors, The* (painting), 57
Hölderlin, Friedrich, 126
Husserl, Edmund, 39, 137, 141, 142, 147

Identity, 37
Illocutionary acts, 78–79, 80, 93
Imagination, 21, 138
Individuality, 9, 49, 87, 143; in Anglo-American and Continental philosophy, 10; authenticity and, 50; effacement of individual, 43; hegemony of the propositional and, 178; Heidegger's rejection of, 101; language in relation of tension with, 149; language's inability to represent, 44, 46–47; propositions and, 88, 89; of speaking subject, 7
Information, 47, 120; intimacy of encounter and, 145, 146; passage of time as, 165; structure of, 8
Instrumentality, *see* Equipmentality (instrumentality)
Intelligibility, 9, 46, 95, 119, 150; anxiety and, 97; content and, 15, 78; of everyday language, 19; facts and, 30, 31, 156; hegemony of propositions and, 29; individuality and, 49; limits of, 14; linguistic community and, 81; as magnetic field, 100; the personal and, 90; poetry and, 104; pragmatic conception of, 80, 91; as public realm, 11–12, 178, 181; subversion of, 54; truth of the individual and, 89
Irony, 14, 63

James, Henry, 3, 149; *Beast in the Jungle, The*, 3, 149
Jay, Martin, 189n19
Judgment: aesthetic, 135–38, 139, 142; cognitive, 8, 29, 32, 36, 138

Kafka, Franz, 58, 62; "Before the Law," 58–60
Kant, Immanuel, 17, 135–41, 143, 161, 162–63; *Critique of Judgment*, 17, 137, 161, 162, 163; *Critique of Pure Reason*, 135
Kenaan, Hagi, 184n2, 186n10, 188n19, 190n20

Kierkegaard, Søren, 9, 16, 55; *Concluding Unscientific Postscript*, 44; *Either/Or*, 41; *Fear and Trembling*, 50, 53n; Hegelian system and, 10; Heidegger compared with, 88–90; on limits of language, 44–45, 48, 49, 53–54; on meaning transcending language, 50–52; on philosophy as disappointment, 41, 42–43, 60–63

Knowledge, sharing of, 8, 27

Kundera, Milan, 112, 115, 116–18, 120; *Unbearable Lightness of Being, The*, 112–22

Language: as action, 85; anonymous, 144, 146; captivity in, 23–24, 36, 43, 54, 89; colloquial, 125–26; contents of, 33; everydayness and, 92; existence beyond, 50–52; experience of, 1–2; facticity of, 14, 90, 156; frame of, 25–28; freedom in, 65; human interaction and, 81, 128; individual's presence in, 1–5; as the Law, 58–60; limits of, 52, 53–58; listening to, 3–4; logos and, 34–36; as map, 44–49; meaning and, 7, 9, 25, 26, 32, 83, 92; the personal in relation to, 97–102, 149–50, 177–82; as phenomenon, 75, 137–38, 140–47, 182; philosophy as disappointment and, 60–63; picture and, 22–23; private, 118; propositional, 36, 39, 60; public and private dimensions of, 2, 7, 134, 179, 180; silence and, 50–52; situatedness of, 85, 91–92; speech act and, 67–68; structure in, 4, 16, 55; suchness of things and, 128; of taste, 138–40; teleology of, 82–83; time and possibility in relation to, 153–58, 173–74; *see also* Philosophy of language; Speech

Legibility, 57, 120

Levinas, Emmanuel, 4, 5

Limits, 44–45, 48, 49, 52, 53–58; content and, 16–17; of intelligibility, 14; of language, 52, 53–58; of philosophy, 43

Listening, 2, 17, 126

Locutionary act, 78, 79

Logos, 19, 34–36

McDowell, John, 8, 47, 70

Marcuse, Herbert, 13, 14; *One-Dimensional Man*, 13

Marxism, 107

Masqueraders, 73

Meaning, 4, 8, 50–52, 107; abstract form of, 5; "as"-structure and, 94; everydayness and, 99, 112, 115; experience and, 11; facts and, 30–31, 45, 51; individuation and, 48; locutionary act and, 78, 79; logos and, 35; multiplicity of, 133; the personal as fabric of, 149; philosophical preface and, 160; positivism and, 29; as "present-at-hand," 91; private, 118–19; propositional form and, 93; public sphere of, 182; repetitive fixation and, 23; self-identity of, 33; speech situation and, 58; teleology of, 141; time and, 117

Memory, 116

Merleau-Ponty, Maurice, 149

Mill, John Stuart, 29

Milosz, Czeslaw, 53

Mind, philosophy of, 6

Mirrors, 24, 84–85

Mitchell, W. J. T., 106

Music, 116, 117–18, 120, 132

Nabokov, Vladimir, 23

Nachman of Bratslav, Rabbi, 179–80

Nietzsche, Friedrich, 11, 12, 183n6; on interpretations versus facts, 31, 39; on positivism, 29–30, 39, 47, 185n14; *Will to Power, The*, 29
Nihilism, 29

Objectivity, 129, 131–33, 136–37
Odysseus, 17
Ontology, 88, 90, 97
Oppenheim, Meret: *Luncheon in Fur*, 112
Ordinary, the, *see* Everydayness (the ordinary)

Paradox, 52, 53, 54
Performative sentences, 69, 71, 72–76, 131; judgment of taste and, 139; linguistic community and, 81; meaning and, 130; primacy of, 84
Personal, the, 4, 55, 177–82; concreteness of, 149; elision of, 9, 97–102; encounter and, 144–46; hidden, 120; intelligibility and, 119; language in relation to, 16, 17, 56–57, 150; listening to, 17; meaning and, 37; pragmatic form and, 79–83; vulnerability of, 5
Perspective, 33, 57, 134, 137
Phenomenology, 17, 137, 141, 178, 179, 186n3; *see also* Husserl, Edmund; Merleau-Ponty, Maurice
Philosophy, 126–27; disappointment and, 41–43; limits of, 43; limits of language and, 54; meaning in, 31; the personal and, 19; philosophical texts, prefaces to, 159–68; reflexivity as captivity, 20–24; speech and, 2, 126
Philosophy of language, 2, 6, 9–10; domination and, 13; history of, 68; pragmatic turn in, 87
Physiognomy, 4

Pictures, 20–24
Plath, Sylvia, 39
Plato, 20, 21, 35, 141; *Sophist*, 34–35; *Symposium*, 141
Poetry, 14, 15, 27, 53, 142; Heidegger and, 100, 101–2, 189n7; intelligibility and, 54, 104; and the ordinary, 121, 122–23; in *Unbearable Lightness of Being*, 121
Positive thinking, 13, 14
Positivism, 29, 30, 47, 107, 185n14
Possibility, 43, 48, 60, 96; in everyday language, 125, 126; passage of time and, 153–58
Poststructuralism, 10
"Pragmatic turn," 68–71
Preface, of philosophy texts, 159–68
Propositional form, 8, 9, 178; frame of language and, 25, 26; hegemony of, 65, 71, 83, 87, 88–89, 95, 134, 140, 178; intelligibility and, 46–47; judgment and, 28–33, 139; meaning and, 33, 37–39, 94; the personal in relation to, 55, 158, 178; singularity and, 157; speech act and, 73; suchness of things and, 34–37
Protest, 13, 14
Psychoanalytic theory, 23

Quine, W. V. O.: *Pursuit of Truth, The*, 161, 162, 165–68; *Word and Object*, 166

Ramsey, Frank, 170
Reflection, 37, 135, 159
Reification, 5, 33
Representation, 66, 70, 104, 108; as action, 84–85; facts and, 80; map as, 44, 45; of reality, 42
Responsibility, 65, 84, 121
Russell, Bertrand, 27–28, 31, 59, 130; *Inquiry into Meaning and Truth, An*,

Russell (*continued*)
27–28, 184n9; "Introduction" to *Tractatus* (Wittgenstein), 27, 184n7; *Philosophy of Logical Atomism, The*, 31
Ryle, Gilbert, 21, 68

Sartre, Jean-Paul, 14, 23
Schapiro, Meyer, 105–9, 189n17; "Still Life as a Personal Object, The: Note on Heidegger and van Gogh," 105–6
Searle, John, 70
Self, 11, 16, 177, 178
Self-alienation, 95
Semantics, 76, 87, 117, 118, 187n11
Sense, taste of, 135
Sentences, 27–28, 72–73, 74, 127–28, 129–30
Silence, 14, 52, 53–54, 97
Singularity, 62, 121, 182; of the individual, 44, 56, 179; meaning of language and, 47
Speech, 2–3, 28, 100; act of, 66, 67–68, 72–79, 81, 92; communicability of artwork, 110–11, 122; construction of, 67; meaningfulness of, 128–29, 130; neutrality of, 82; philosophy of language and, 8; situation of, 68, 82; standard versus "special," 33; thematization of, 75–76; *see also* Language
Spencer, Herbert, 29
Sraffa, P., 170
Strawson, Peter, 69
Structure, in language, 4, 54, 55, 56, 60, 69
Subjectivity, 10, 14, 129, 132, 141; aesthetic judgment and, 135, 137; beauty and, 140

Taste, judgment of, 135–40
Temporality, 33, 155, 165, 166, 170

Textuality, 109, 111
Thought, space of, 31
Time, 150–52, 168–74; language and, 153–59; in philosophical prefaces, 159–68; possibility and, 153–58, 174–76
Totality, 111, 173
Trakl, Georg: "Winter Evening," 101
Transcendence, 33, 63
Truth, 27, 28, 31, 32, 107; art as occurrence of, 103; expressivity and, 130; facts and, 156–57; individuality and, 89; language opposed to, 98; performatives and, 74; philosophy as disappointment and, 42–43; suchness of things and, 129

Universality, 135–36, 137, 159
Utterances, 70, 75, 76, 79; expressivity of, 130; intersubjectivity and, 143; as objective and subjective, 132–33, 190n5; performativity of, 131; suchness of things and, 128

Valéry, Paul, 15, 191n1
Van Gogh, Vincent, 102–11, 112
Verbs, 35
Vermeer, Jan, 149
Vienna Circle, 53

Wittgenstein, Ludwig, 4, 30, 63, 68, 128; Anglo-American philosophy and, 87; Austin compared with, 73; fly-in-bottle analogy, 6, 55–56; frame of language and, 25–26, 34; on Kierkegaard, 53–54; on the limits of language, 16; on music and language, 120; *Philosophical Investigations*, 20, 21, 25, 26, 151, 168–74; on philosophical reflection as captivity, 20–24; on philosophy and the everyday, 85; on propositions, 29; Quine compared with, 165, 167, 168; on suchness of things, 36; on time passing, 150–52, 153, 156–58, 161, 164, 168–74; *Tractatus Logico-Philosophicus*, 25, 151, 169, 172, 191*n*3